COOK DOWN CHOLESTEROL

The Silk Road to Health

Blog: cooks2books.blogspot.com
Facebook: cooks2books
cooks2books@gmail.com

List of contributors:

Annie Allerdice, Graphic Artist
Mary Bartlett, Editing
Sue Carmody, Recipes, Editing, Photography
Chester D. Dog, Taster
Marcus Dougherty, Table Accessories
Terry Erfeldt, Recipe Testing, Editing
Leslie Gatton, Editing and Ideas
Brandon Hanson, Ideas
Miles Hassell, MD, Encourgement
Arlene Holmes, Editing
Kathleen Mullane, Cheerleader
Holly Pence, Editor Extraordinaire
Lloyd Warnes, Table Accessories
Kate Welsh, Consultant
Megan Sage, Editing
Nancy Wirsig, Graphic Artist, hand2mouse.com
Elliot Zais, Recipe Testing, Recipe Writing, Editor Extraordinaire

Without all of the above contributors, this cookbook would not have been possible. I remain forever grateful.

About the Author

Sheila Hanson grew up in a small town north of Chicago. Her mother was a very plain cook with one thought in mind, "when it's smokin' it's cookin', when it's burned, it's done." From an early age Sheila sought ways to improve her dining fare. Attempting to cook chewing gum so it would be softer to chew, the effort ended in major burns on her hand when trying to catch it before it landed on the floor. This did not deter her never ending quest for food that not only tasted good, but was good for the body and good for the soul.

After raising three children, she attended the Culinary Institute of America in Hyde Park, NY and Napa Valley, CA. Ms. Hanson spent over 20 years managing food service operations in colleges, schools, retirement centers and private clubs. She is currently an instructor for cooking classes and food styling.

About the Assistant Author

Chester, a Cavalier King Charles Spaniel, was born near Tucson, AZ. At the age of three, his owner became allergic to him and had to give him up. Finding himself unemployed, he moved to Portland and became the chef's helper and assistant author. He has books and cartoons written about him that are yet to be published, along with restaurant reviews he personally crafted. However, he generously put those "works in progress" aside to assist with this cookbook.

COOK
DOWN
CHOLESTEROL

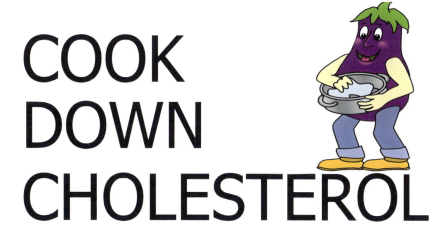

The Silk Road to Health

Sheila Hanson

Cavalier Digital Media
Portland, Oregon

FIRST EDITION 2010

Book Design by Sheila Hanson

Cover by Nancy Wirsig McClure, hand2mouse.com
Title Page Illustration by Nancy Wirsig McClure, hand2mouse.com

Interior Photographs by Sheila Hanson
Interior Illustrations by Annie Allerdice, Nancy Wirzig McClure and Sheila Hanson

To my dear husband and best friend,
George Hanson

No matter what you eat

the telling is in your health...

CONTENTS

Forward

For those of us who wish to avoid heart disease and stroke in your futures, it pays to constantly remind ourselves that the most important steps we must take are daily exercise and prudent food choices. By prudent food choices, we mean a whole-food Mediterranean-style diet, which so far is the only dietary pattern with substantial evidence for reducing common chronic diseases, including ischemic heart disease. Defining the whole-food Mediterranean diet need not get too complicated. Emphasizing vegetables, fruit, beans, and whole grains is a good start, as well as 'healthy fats' such as extra-virgin olive oil, avocado, raw nuts, and fish. Add some variety with moderate amounts of dairy, meat, and poultry, and avoid preserved (processed) meats, hydrogenated oils, sweets, sweet drinks, and white flour.

Having done all that, you'll probably notice an improved sense of well being, some weight loss, lower blood pressure, and some small improvements in your cholesterol, particularly in your HDL (High Density Lipoprotein) cholesterol, sometimes called 'good cholesterol'. However, particularly for those who already have heart disease, you may be looking to lower your LDL cholesterol further than we would expect to see with a typical whole food Mediterranean diet. Often we use medicines – such as 'statin' drugs – for that purpose, but many people wish to minimize their use of medicines and emphasize the foods known to lower cholesterol.

This is where Sheila Hanson's book may be able to help. *Cook Down Cholesterol, The Silk Road to Health* features numerous foods that are not only healthy, but are particularly good for reducing your LDL cholesterol. Often overlooked, like okra and eggplant, they typically lower cholesterol through various forms of fiber they contain, which work in the intestines to increase the excretion of cholesterol from your body. So keep reading, and learn more about these foods and ways to include them in your diet.

Miles Hassell, M.D.
Internal Medicine
Comprehensive Risk Reduction Clinic
Portland, OR
www.goodfoodgreatmedicine.com

Preface

I was driven to write this book because my cholesterol was at an all time high of 419. My doctor had been after me to get it down. I tried Pravachol, Lipitor, and a niacin combo. All of these produced side effects that made me feel dreadful. My hair was falling out. I had triple vision - an indication that there was a brain problem not an eye problem. I was considering giving up night driving and was limiting my day time driving because I just couldn't see very well.

After investigating the information about side effects from these medications, I discovered I was having SIDE EFFECTS. I got off the medication with my doctor's help and took a second look at the suggestion sheet he gave me. The ingredients for lowering cholesterol were okra, eggplant, nutritional brewers yeast, flax seed and soy lecithin. I was intrigued by these ingredients. I knew about okra, but eggplant and what to do with it—was another puzzle to be put together. As for the other ingredients, I had no idea what to do with them or where to buy them.

My food background consists of attending the Culinary Institute of America in Hyde Park, NY and Napa Valley, CA. I spent 20 years managing food service in retirement homes, retreat centers, schools and private clubs. I knew I had to write a cookbook that made lowering cholesterol easy and delicious.

I have a passion for the history of vegetables, herbs and spices which led to making this cookbook a virtual trip along the Silk Road seeking information that would reveal a diet delicious in flavor and bringing the needed health benefits.

A quick glance through the book reveals the ease of cooking delicious foods that can make a difference in your cholesterol levels.

CHAPTER 1
The Silk Road to Health

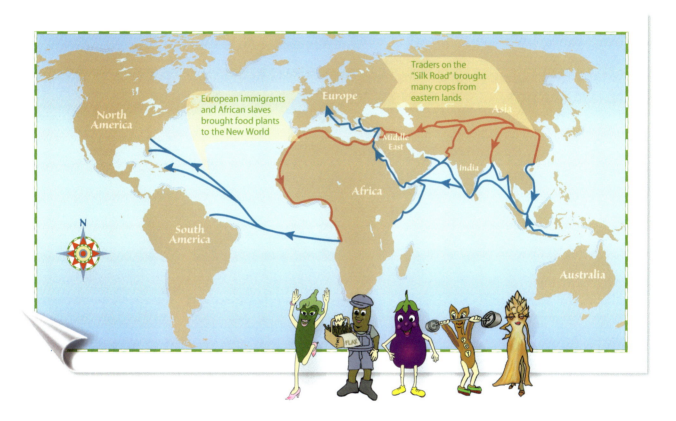

Traders on the "Silk Road" brought many crops from eastern lands

European immigrants and African slaves brought food plants to the New World

North America

Europe

Asia

Middle East

India

Africa

South America

Australia

N

The Silk Road is an extensive network of trade routes across the Asian continent connecting East, South, and Western Asia with the Mediterranean world, North and Northeast Africa, and Europe. As the Silk Road developed, vegetables and seeds began their journey to our table.

When I began researching the Silk Road, I thought the Silk Road only carried silk or tea. Well, enterprising people and their beasts of burden actually carried merchandise of all kinds back and forth on the Silk Road. Veggies and seeds were a major industry themselves. The quantities of agriculture transported on the Silk Road quietly impacted the world more than silk or tea. Hmmm, that shouldn't really be much of a surprise: Everybody eats.

The map above includes the routes taken by some of the first vegetables and seeds to arrive in the Americas.

Perhaps the Silk Road should have a been called the Vast Veggie Path. However, a nineteenth century geographer named it *The Silk Road* on the maps he drew and the name stuck.

Religion played a part in the distribution of vegetables and seeds. The Moors took them along on their quest to spread the Muslim religion. The Crusades transported them on their journey to the Holy Land.

Vegetables and seeds traveled with traders and religious groups to the northern coast of Africa. Vegetables and seeds managed to find their way south and west in Africa as groups pursued their professions. People returning or retreating north to Italy, northwest to Spain and on to the British Isles did their part in spreading vegetables and seeds.

Christopher Columbus was the first European to bring vegetables and seeds to America. In a manner of speaking, extending The Silk Road to the New World.

Vegetables and seeds, even in ancient times, didn't seem to be as highly prized as silk or tea. There were salt wars, but I haven't read about any massacres over carrots. Vegetables and seeds hitchhiked around the world quietly feeding the masses.

When you begin your cooking journey on *The Silk Road to Health*, you'll indulge in mouth-watering entrees, delicious side dishes and decadent desserts while lowering your cholesterol.

Lowering LDL ("Bad") Cholesterol With Food
By Miles Hassell, MD

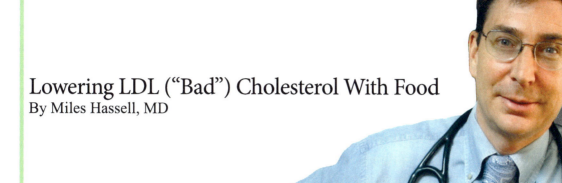

Control your LDL (bad) cholesterol

Goal: LDL of less than 160 mg/dl in low risk patients, and less than 100 mg/dl or even 70 mg/dl in high-risk patients (Ask your doctor what your target should be.)

Low-density lipoprotein (LDL) is a form of cholesterol strongly related to increased risk of heart disease, particularly in those who have other risk factors for heart disease. Although controlling LDL is important, don't rely solely on a low LDL to prevent a heart attack: most people who have heart attacks in the US are already at their recommended LDL goal.[1]

There are many drugs I use to lower LDL cholesterol. However, with consistent use of food choices you may not need medications at all, or you may get by with a smaller dose of medication, reducing expense and side-effects.

Mediterranean diet and LDL

In studies using the Mediterranean diet without the goal of lowering LDL, the LDL may stay the same or fall up to 10 percent. More importantly, the Mediterranean diet is associated with a reduction in LDL oxidation, a benefit which may be more important than simply lowering the total amount of LDL.

Some foods to lower LDL

When assessing the LDL-lowering effects of food, compare the expected effect with the fact that doubling any given dose of a statin drug will typically lower your LDL by only another 6 – 9 percent. Many patients use the foods mentioned on the following page in order to keep their statin dose low. LDL-lowering foods can easily be incorporated into your diet, and each could typically lower LDL by 5 – 10 percent. Using several measures together can lower your LDL cholesterol up to 30 percent, an effect similar to that of a medium dose of a statin drug.

These LDL-lowering foods can also lower your triglycerides, raise HDL, improve your blood sugar control, and are associated with lower levels of inflammation. The more of these steps you take, the more of an improvement you will see in your LDL.

These foods do not work for everyone, unfortunately, but they can have some amazing results. A couple of our patients have seen their LDL cholesterol drop by 50 percent with the vigorous use of these foods. The higher your LDL, the better these foods work. Give any food program about 6 weeks to work.

---

1 Sachdeva A et al, Am Heart J 2009;157:111-17

• Psyllium (e.g. Metamucil) to lower LDL

A daily dose of 10 grams psyllium (about 2 heaping teaspoons) can sometimes reduce LDL by about 7 percent.[2] In some studies, psyllium has failed to lower LDL but has had a beneficial effect in raising HDL and lowering triglycerides.[3] Most people stir psyllium into water or juice. A method that works well is to stir it into a small amount of water, drink it quickly before it gels, and then follow with 12 ounces of water. Psyllium is a great anti-constipation agent, too.

• Oat Bran to lower LDL

Using 4 tablespoons (¼ cup) of oat bran each day may give about 10 – 26 percent reduction in LDL.[4] Oat bran can be added to cereal, stirred into yogurt or smoothies, or added to muffins.

• Raw almonds to lower LDL

About two handfuls of raw almonds (about 30 almonds or two ounces) daily can reduce LDL by 9 percent. Raw walnuts, hazelnuts, Brazil nuts, and pecans probably work as well. Adding raw nuts to your diet also has the important benefit of reducing oxidized LDL as well as another risk factor called Lp(a).[5] (See *Heart disease risk factors not discussed in this chapter* on page 41.)

• Eggplant and okra to lower LDL

About 6 ounces of eggplant or about 3 – 4 ounces of okra every other day can also lower LDL. These foods have not been studied by themselves, but when used in combination with other factors, have been found to lower LDL by 28 percent. Inflammation was reduced as well.[6]

• Soy and other beans to lower LDL

Soy foods modestly reduce cholesterol. These are probably best included in the diet in the form of whole traditional soy foods such as soybeans (edamame), tofu, miso, and tempeh. I am less enthusiastic about the highly refined soy products like soy milk. For those who use soy milk because of dairy intolerance, read the ingredient label carefully. Some other beans also lower LDL to a similar degree, particularly pinto beans. A half-cup of cooked pinto beans or 25 grams of soy protein will lower LDL 5 percent or more.[7]

• Stanols to lower LDL

There are a variety of stanol-containing margarines that can lower LDL cholesterol. I don't tend to recommend them because of concerns over the problems with hydrogenated oils in the margarine, and the debate over whether stanols at these doses have potential for harm.[8] Time will tell.

Medications to lower LDL

Most people who need significant LDL lowering are also likely to need prescription medication, usually a statin. However, some people are able to control their cholesterol with a whole food diet enhanced on a daily basis with the foods described above. (See *addendum* for Dr. Hassell's update)

2   Am. J. Clin. Nutr. 2000;71:472-9
3   Sola, R.Am J Clin Nutr 2007;85:1157-63
4   JACN 1998;17:601-608
5   Circulation 2002;106:1327-32
6   Jenkins JAMA 2003;290:502-510

7   Winham DM et al. JACN 2007;26:243-9
8   Fransen J Nutrition 2007;137:1301-

Dr. Jacobus Rinse

Dr. Hassell suggested I use the *Rinse Formula* along with eggplant, okra. and a few nuts daily as a snack.

The rinse part of this diet is named after a chemist, Jocabus Rinse, who had an attack of angina pectoris at the age of 51. He investigated the possible reasons for these attacks and concluded that diet played a large roll in the problem.

Dr. Rinse's hypothesis was that there was a deficiency in his diet. He believed the human body is like a chemical energy plant producing various kinds of energies for moving and thinking, for electric energy and for heat. A chemical plant needs primary as well as secondary materials to operate efficiently and effectively. The ingredients in Dr. Rinse's formula reflect the vitamins and minerals that may be missing in people with high cholesterol.

Rinse Formula

1 Tablespoon Granular Soy Lecithin
1 Tablespoon Nutritional Brewers Yeast
2 Tablespoons Whole Flaxseed

Use the *Rinse Formula* on most days.

Also include OATS, OAT BRAN, and brown rice as much as possible.

I adjusted the ingredients to accommodate my allergies. This formula reduced my cholesterol in 21 days from 419 to 271.

See addendum for Dr. Hassell's update on Dr. Jacobus Rinse's formula and nutrition information.
Ref: The Journal of the American Oil Chemists Society article, " Atherosclerosis, Chemistry, and Nutrition," by Dr. J. Rinse American Laboratory July 1973

CHAPTER 2

OKRA

Oddball Okra

The wiley okra and its slime
Has finally come into its time
Who woulda thunk the fuzzy pod
Would harbor health from neath the sod

China or Africa from whence it came
Remains a mystery all the same
The silk road travel that it took
Brought many foods for us to cook

No wars we know have ere been fought
But its journey was not for naught
So many uses can be found
Like soups or sauces that abound

Okra takes a stand at last
For recognition and repast
Follow closely and you will find
Health and flavor all combined

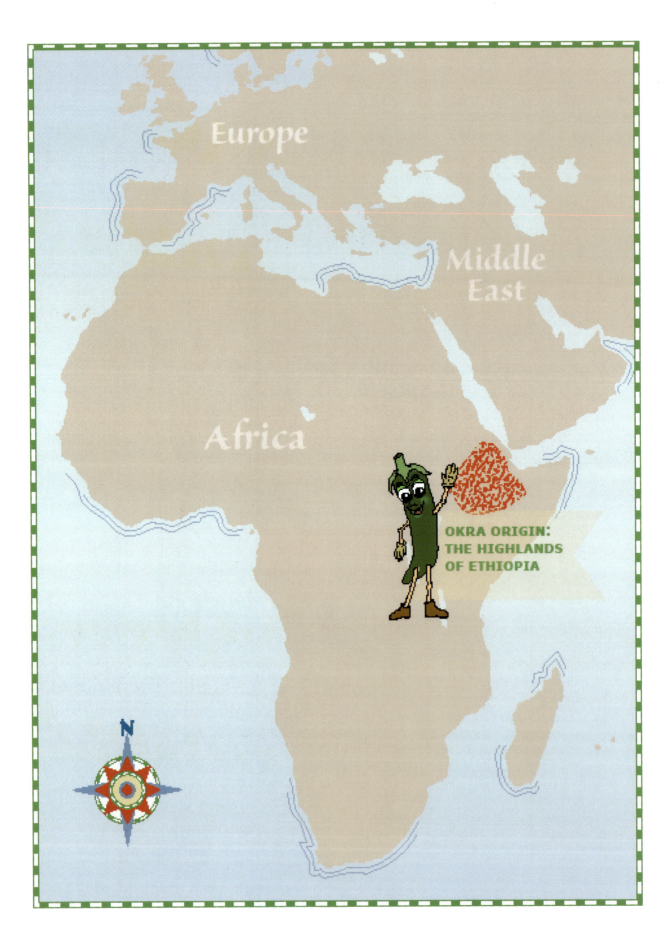

Okra

Research indicates okra originated in the Ethiopian highlands in Africa. While not exactly traveling on the original Silk Road, these vegetable vagabonds found their way to North America by traveling to the west coast of Africa and eventually across the Atlantic Ocean.

Some history books say the French colonists brought okra to other parts of the world and somehow to North America. Perhaps their ability to read and write allowed them to publish records making it easy to make that claim. Most accounts credit the slaves for its arrival in America. Hmmm, could it be a combination? Did the French grab the glory simply because they could read and write and the slaves couldn't? There is lots of conjecture about this marvelous little pod.

Okra is a slippery fellow and often gets an bad rap. It has a subtle sweet flavor that would remind you of eggplant. When cooked into a dish, okra turns silky and gives the most pleasant "mouth feel." *Once you learn to cook with it, you'll enjoy the subtle flavor and texture it adds while helping to lower cholesterol.*

Growing your own okra in the Northwest is arduous. The season is short and it is difficult to pick. Their redeeming fact is they do produce a beautiful bloom, interesting leaves and a tasty healthy vegetable. It is not in season for very long each summer. So for the most part frozen sliced or frozen whole okra works just fine in the recipes.

Most people think okra is only used in gumbo or battered and deep fried. Not so, as you'll see in the recipes that follow. Much like it's helpful mate, the eggplant, it is easily slipped into any dish to add flavor, texture and health benefits. The valuable nutrients, nearly half of which are soluble fiber, are in the form of gums and pectins. Soluble fiber helps to lower serum cholesterol. The other half is insoluble fiber which helps to keep the intestinal tract healthy decreasing the risk of some forms of cancer, especially colorectal cancer. Nearly 10% of the recommended levels of vitamin B6 and folic acid are also present in a half cup of cooked okra. (ref.: http://urbanext.illinois.edu/veggies/okra1.html)

I suggest you begin eating it in gumbos. When you get used to it in gumbos, you may want to experiment like I did. I bought some whole okra and put it into a beef stew. I found great pleasure in putting the whole okra in my mouth and popping it. Feeling those little seeds explode is a thrill to the palate all in itself. Caution! (work your way up to the whole pod pop!

After much research into the travels of the slippery little pod, the "Great Okra Route" really remains a mystery. It's difficult to imagine nations fighting wars over okra the way they did over tea. Now that people are beginning to harbor health related thoughts about okra, could it be time to invest in okra futures?

Okra Handling and Prep

There isn't much to say about the handling of okra other than open the bag of frozen okra, either whole or sliced, and pour. Very simple.

I don't recommend fresh okra as it is too time consuming and fresh okra either isn't available or the quality isn't good in many parts of the country. The Pacific Northwest is especially barren of good okra. I believe the poor quality of the Pacific Northwest okra comes from cool summer nights. Other parts of the country grow excellent okra, so I say "Let 'em." Buy okra frozen for the very best product. Fred Meyer grocery store has about the best okra in the Portland area.

Cooking okra can be a slippery slope. I like to compare it to silky threads of nutrition. Unless you really enjoy the silky texture of okra, it is more palatable when mixed with something like tomatoes, sauerkraut, or milk to name a few. It needs an acid type companion to control the "silk." I've incorporated delightful okra into as many recipes as possible because it has a heavenly flavor and texture when handled properly.

Don't be intimated by the silkiness, be bold, try it in a gumbo to begin with, and I know you'll enjoy it more and more as you cook with it.

My daddy loved okra and would fix a nice big pot of it. It took my growing up and classes at the N'Orleans School of Cooking to learn to use and enjoy it. Follow the tongue smacking recipes and find yourself in finger-licking heaven.

Okra Nutrition

One cup of OKRA contains 34 CALORIES while delivering protein, calcium, iron, magnesium, phosphorus, potassium, zinc, manganese, thiamin, riboflavin, niacin, vitamin A, vitamin E, beta carotene, lutein + zeaxanthin to name a few. For a full description go to the USDA website. http://www.nal.usda.gov/fnic/food-comp/search/ The website takes a little fiddling with to get it to work, but well worth the trouble. If you have questions, email them and they respond quickly.

USDA ** Percent Daily Values are based on a 2,000 calorie diet. Your daily values maybe higher or lower depending on your calorie needs.

Chapter 3

EGGPLANT

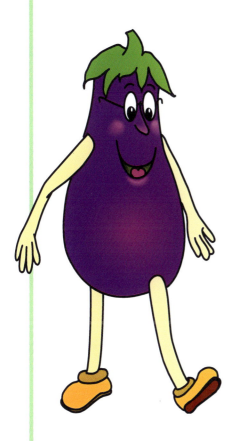

The Mighty Eggplant

The mighty eggplant makes the scene
With many shapes and colored sheen
Is there sex or gender there?
Doesn't' matter - just prepare

Skin on or off can be a query
With responses and a theory
Does it matter all that much
It's all a question worth a touch

Don't let this veggie be so daunting
It's got the stuff that's worth flaunting
You'll have the answers that you seek
For cholesterol without a peak
Oh triglycerides of scary number
That keep us from our needed slumber

From the depths beneath the skin
Comes a formula from within
All the recipes you will see
Begin to solve the mystery

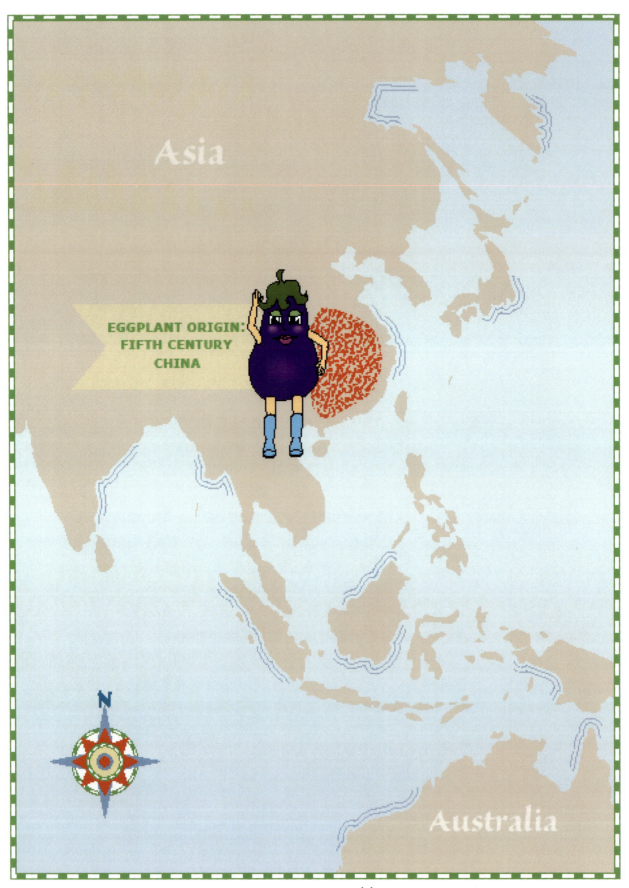

Eggplant

The origin of eggplant is a bit vague. It is thought eggplant may have its origins in India, but early written accounts from a 5th century Chinese record on agriculture indicated cultivation began in China.

Thomas Jefferson gets the credit for the introduction of eggplant to North America. Eggplant was seldom heard of or cultivated much in the U. S. until about 1950. It's a solid member of the nightshade family and related to the potato and tomato. Other parts of the world call the eggplant aubergine, brinjal, melanzana, garden egg, and patlican. This vegetable beauty comes in multiple shapes and colors. Eggplant can be eaten with or without the skin.

Needless to say, eggplants are more readily available in the summer. Some times of the year it is nearly impossible to get a good eggplant. New Seasons grocery stores in Portland, OR seem to be one of the few stores that consistently has fresh eggplants year round. I don't understand why it is not available frozen in the grocery stores. Eggplant is simple to freeze. It blends with nearly every dish you want to prepare and brings untold health benefits. Eggplant adds a lovely texture to any dish. I use grilled eggplant in recipes to replace mushrooms. To me, the flavor and texture are similar.

Eggplant is often found in Indian cooking. It can be added to nearly any soup, stew, casserole dish, and perhaps a chutney. The newly-found health benefits should be a good reason to include this likeable veg in any meal.

For a year, I spent hours, days and weeks carefully developing eggplant recipes. Then, on New Years Day, when I was sick and tired of cooking, chopping and even eating food in general, I looked at the eggplant and hacked it in half, then in half again and plopped it on the grill. It was delightful and the lovely subtle nutty flavor rang through. Hmmmm, what a treat and there was no muss or fuss. Simple can often be the best. My menu was roast duck (with nothing on it), cooked eggplant for the salad, and okra, onions and rice for the combined vegetable and starch.

Probably the best way to start out eating it is to sauce it, casserole it, and/or disguise it any way that seems like *it* might taste good. After you've disguised it by all of these mentioned treatments, try it simply quartered, brushed with olive oil and grilled or baked. The flavor is magnificent. I've included a salad recipe that uses no oil either.

Eggplant is a great accompaniment to duck or, actually, nearly anything you can think of that needs some company. So, remember, don't bury this little gem under sauces, herbs and spices–it's good enough to stand on its own. Eggplant's simple splendor will enhance any plate and add to the ambience, flavor and health of meals.

Eggplant Handling and Prep

To cook or not to cook... COOK, always COOK
Do not, under any circumstances, eat raw eggplant. Results will be a tummy ache on steroids.

To salt or not to salt...

Most recipes call for sprinkling salt on the eggplant, let drain for 30 minutes, rinse and pat dry with paper towels. The theory behind salting is to remove water from the eggplant. Wow, that's a lot of work and waste of paper towels to say nothing of adding salt. We certainly don't need more salt in our diets. There is no need to remove the water. Keeping produce as close to it's original form as possible is the best way to maintain its flavor and nutritional integrity.

To peel or not to peel...

Peeling or not peeling, it's your choice. If your lower digestive tract is sensitive, then by all means PEEL. Otherwise the added fiber is a good thing and helps retain more nutrients.

Freeze:

In general, vegetables must be heated before freezing to maintain the integrity of flavor, texture, and nutrition. There is a recipe for freezing eggplant in the recipe section of this book. For complete information on preserving food products, I've found googling the most useful tool to look up information. Go to the Google search engine and type in: USDA: preserving vegetables

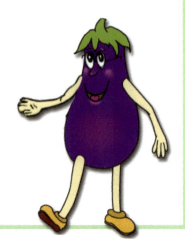

EGGPLANT NUTRITION

One cup of eggplant contains 20 CALORIES with small amounts of protein, a few carbs, some calcium, potassium, phosphorus, magnesium, and zinc to name a few. It also contains these vitamins in small amounts:

Folate and vitamin A among other trace amounts of Thiamin, Riboflavin, Niacin, Pantothenic acid, Vitamin B-6.

For a full description go to the USDA website:http://www.nal.usda.gov/fnic/foodcomp/ search/ The website takes a little fiddling with to get it to work, but well worth the trouble.

USDA ** Percent Daily Values are based on a 2,000 calorie diet. Your daily values maybe higher or lower depending on your calorie needs.

Eggplant Chopping

1. If using a light weight chopping board, anchor the chopping board by placing a damp paper towel or damp cloth under the chopping board. This will keep the chopping board from slipping while chopping.

2. Begin by washing the eggplant and then removing stem end and any label that might be stuck on the outside. Peel if desired.

3. Place eggplant on chopping board. Cut in half lengthwise. Then, depending on the size cube desired, cut the slices lengthwise creating sticks. Stack evenly.

4. Carefully cut crosswise down through all the slices at intervals large enough to make the desired size cube.

5. While holding all the slices together, carefully cut down through all the slices crosswise at intervals, depending on the size cube desired.

Chapter 4
OATS

Lady Oat

Oats in our meals
Provide good deals
They bring us the bulk we need
Such a deal and cheap indeed

Food for a horse you may say
Good replacement for some hay
Think again you dear ol' soul
Good health for life should be your goal

Grab your spoon or your cracker
This mighty oat is not a slacker
With not much work or added sweat
It's the best food you can get

USDA ** Percent Daily Values are based on a 2,000 calorie diet. Your daily values maybe higher or lower depending on your calorie needs.

21

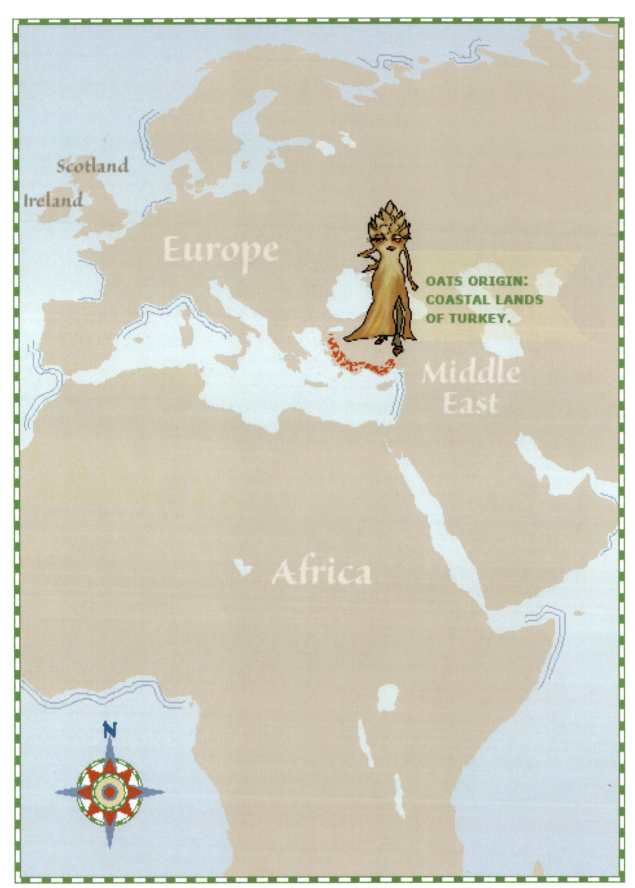

OATS ORIGIN: COASTAL LANDS OF TURKEY.

Scotland

Ireland

Europe

Middle East

Africa

Oats

Oats began their march to the western world from Asia Minor which roughly corresponds to modern-day Turkey. The Aegean and Mediterranean sea coasts have cool, rainy winters and hot, moderately dry summers. Cool moist climates provide the best growing conditions. Oats are often associated with the British Isles, and especially with Scotland and Ireland. The oat came to this country in the late 1600's but was mainly grown for animal feed. In the last few years, health aficionados latched on to them as a key to lowering cholesterol. Even so, only five per cent of Americans eat oats in one form or another. How sad for us as it is not only extremely healthy, but cheap and not all that difficult to cook. Oats are not a crop you can easily plant and harvest yourself, so just pay attention to how to use it for maximum benefits.

One of England's best known literary figures, Samuel Johnson (1709-1784), defined oats as "eaten by people in Scotland, but fit only for horses in England." A Scotsman replied, "That's why England has such good horses, and Scotland has such fine men!"

In the olden days in Scotland, every croft (homestead) had its own girnel (oatmeal barrel), as well as a porridge drawer. A batch of porridge would be made at the beginning of the week and kept cold in the drawer so that family members could slice off chunks as needed, perhaps for a snack while working out on the fields. Today, a similar thing could be done by preparing oats and keeping them in the fridge until needed.

The more I find out about oats, the more fascinating they become. The whole oat comes with a hull that has to be removed to reveal the oat groat. Originally I thought there were only rolled oats that came in a box with the picture of the nice portly looking Quaker on the front. I spent many hours playing with those boxes as a child. Now I'm finding oats actually come in other forms that are much better for you and tastier too. With help from this information you can transform your eating and health patterns to a higher plane.

Oat Flower

Oak Spikelet

Green Oats

Fuzzy Oat Flower

Photography: Oat flower, oat spikelet and fuzzy oat flower pictures courtesy of Iowa State University. Green oats: Sheila Hanson

Oat Groats would remind you of wheat kernels. The outer covering is the bran which is touted as a great source of fiber. One ounce of groats has twice the amount of protein as wheat or corn flakes. Cooked oat groats can be tossed into any dish of the day. They're a tasty breakfast plain or with your favorite topping. Add cooked oat groats to a salad or use at dinner time to replace 'tators or rice. There are several recipes featuring oat groats in the recipe section. Oat groats are under-rated, under-used and under-appreciated.

Steel Cut Oats are oat groats that are cut with steel blades into three or four pieces. They have the same nutrition content as oat groats. They cook a little quicker and deliver a smoother textured product. Steel cuts sound like a lot of work and fuss for a bowl of mush. NOT SO! The glycemic index indicates that oats groats digest more slowly. For a small investment of time, you can reap a harvest of huge health results and wonderful flavors. Oats can add gusto and nutrition to an otherwise boring meal pattern. Oats are NOT just for breakfast, as you'll see in the recipe section.

Rolled Oats are either whole or steel cut groats steamed then passed through rollers to mash them to the manufacturer's specs. This process produces many forms of instant oats. Remember, the more processing that happens, the less nutrition is left. Often nutrition is lost in the processing and the manufacturer artificially adds a small amount back. However, you can "roll" your own oats simply by putting them through an oat rolling machine that is either hand cranked or electric. The machines are available at Bob's Red Mill.

Oat Bran is produced by passing the groats through a series of roller mills and sifters to remove the bran from the floury part of the groat. Oat bran is a very good fiber source. There are many delicious ways to incorporate oat bran into your daily food. You'll find exciting and innovative recipes in this cookbook. Oat bran can be used to thicken soups, as a crust for casseroles, or a to add crispy coating to chicken or fish. There are so many ways to use it that I may write a cookbook just about oats and bran.

All other OATS, meaning quick cooking and/or instant oats, are hardly worth mentioning. They are a waste of time, money, and calories. Spend a few minutes of your day cooking and eating something good for you. Your health is the most important thing you can have some control over. Treat yourself well.

Ref: oat information: www.namamillers.org/

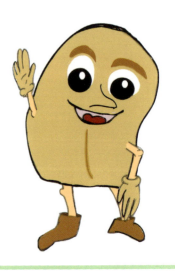

COMPARE OATS VS. QUICK COOKING/INSTANT OATS

Oat groats at about 75¢ a pound with 8 servings to the pound comes out to about 9¢ a serving. Looking at the cost of Instant Oats at a chain grocery store gave me a quick start for sure. A punch in the pocketbook would be the best description. Quick Oats gives all of their benefits to corporate America and little to you. This is one time it would pay to be groaty.

It's difficult to fully compare these two products, because Instant Oats only list the ingredients and not the amount of nutrition. The sugar is natural in the oat groats and ¼ teaspoon is tiny compared to 2 teaspoons in the Quick Oats version of health. The salt and sugar comparisons are frightening.

OAT GROATS

9¢/serving

88 Calories

Servings: ½ cup

Whole oat groats

Calcium (mg)	11
Carbohydrate (g)	13.53
Copper (mg)	0.069
Fat, total (g)	1.27
Fiber, total dietary (g)	2
Folate, total (mcg)	6
Iron (mg)	0.85
Lutein + zeaxanthin (mcg)	36
Magnesium (mg)	30
Monounsaturated fatty acids, total (g)	0.4
Niacin (mg)	0.158
Phosphorus (mg)	96
Potassium (mg)	71
Protein (g)	3.23
Riboflavin (mg)	0.028
Saturated fatty acids, total (g)	0.224
Selenium (mcg)	6.9
Sodium (mg)	1
Sugars, total	**¼ tsp**
Thiamin (mg)	0.147
Vitamin B-6 (mg)	0.024
Vitamin E, alpha tocopherol (mg)	0.14
Vitamin K (mcg)	0.6
Zinc (mg)	0.62

INSTANT OATS

$1.35/serving

200 Calories

Servings: ½ cup

Whole Grain Rolled Oats (with Oat Bran)
Sugar, 2 teaspoons
Artificial Flavors
Salt
Calcium Carbonate (a source of cacium)
Soy Lecithin
Guar Gum
Carmel Color
Niacinamide (One of the B Vitamins)
Vitamin A Palmitate
Reduced Iron,
Pyridoxine Hydrochloride (One of the B   Vitamins)
Riboflavin (One of the B Vitamins)
Thiamin Mononitrate (One of the B Vitamins)
Folic Acid (One of the B Vitamins).

Oat groats 1 lb 75¢
Rolled oats 1 lb 91¢

Quick Oatmeal
 1 serving $1.35

Supermarket brands of quick oatmeal has added sugar that increases the calorie count. I prefer no added sugar or add fresh fruit to sweeten. Put the rolled oats into a thermos with hot water before going to bed. They'll be ready and waiting for you to embrace their goodness before galloping into your day. If you're going to cook them before stepping into the shower in the morning, watch them the first few times you cook them so you don't end up with a nasty burned pan to clean. Blackened oats are not that great and a burned pan is just darned annoying. With a little practice, you will get really good at preparing them using any method you choose. The taste and nutritional value is fabulous.

Oat Meal Recipe
½ cup rolled oats
1   cup boiling
     water

The night before, into preheated thermos place the oatmeal, pour in the water, put on the cap.
the next morning you're ready for breakfast.

Stove-top Oat Groats

¼ cup groats, rinsed
1 cup water
Dash of salt

In small saucepan combine the oats, water and salt. Bring to boil, reduce heat to simmer. Cook until tender about 20 - 30 minutes

Cooking directions from the label of packaged quick oatmeal

Microwave Cooking Directions:
1. Remove lid completely.
2. Add water to dashed line on inside of cup.
3. Stir well.
4. Microwave on High 1 minute to 1minute 15 seconds. Stir.

Microwave ovens vary in rate of heating. Times given are based on 1100- watt ovens.

Hot Water Directions:
1. Remove lid completely.
2. Add boiling water to just below the dashed line on inside of cup.
3. Stir well.

It has been suggested microwaving may destroy valuable nutrition.

To be a true oat aficionado, you need a spurtle. In fact, there is a championship porridge contest held in the fall in Carrbridge, Inverness-Shire, Scotland. Take a look at the Golden Spurtle website: www.goldenspurtle.com/

A spurtle is a marvelous stick shaped like a 12 inch baseball bat. It is invaluable when stirring oatmeal or stew to avoid smashing the ingredients.

Portland Oregon's Bob's Red Mill entered the contest for the first time this year and won first place. I feel so fortunate to live a short distance from Bob's Red Mill.

One of my dreams is to go to Scotland and enter the porridge contest. Imagine showing up and making porridge with pomegranates, rolled into oat groat balls or stir fried with okra?

I've ordered several spurtles from this website in Vermont:

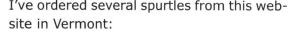
www.piecesofvermont.com
After you get to the website search for spurtle.

From the Scottish National Dictionary Association are some of my favorite terms referring to oats:

- **crackins** a dish of fried oatmeal.
- **creeshie mealie** oatmeal fried in fat.
- **crowdie**, oatmeal and water mixed and eaten raw.
- **kail (English Kale) brose** brose made with the liquid from boiled kail.
- **neep brose** brose made with the liquid in which turnips have been boiled.
- **purry** a savoury dish consisting of oatmeal brose with chopped kail stirred into it.
- **skink** a kind of thin, oatmeal-and-water gruel.
- **snap & rattle** toasted oatcakes crumbled in milk.

CHAPTER 5
SOY BEANS
SOY LECITHIN

Soy Beans

So many things this plant provides
Health returns it's surface hides
The little thing like lecithin
Imparts its goodness from within

Where would we be without this bean
Not so many of us would be seen
It feeds the world in many ways
With healthy bites set onto trays

It's whirled and spun and even quakes
Then heated or frozen that's what it takes
To give the world a diverse cuisine
Fit for children, king or queen

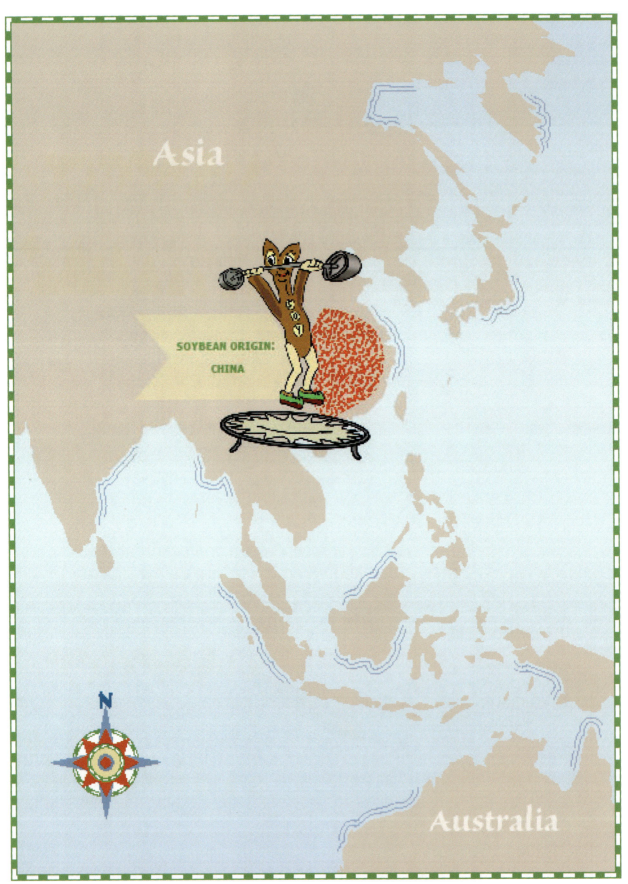

Soy Beans - Soy Lecithin

Soy lecithin comes from the soy bean. Once again we look to China as the origin of soy beans. There are more than 10,000 varieties of these nutrition filled little fellows. Soy beans first arrived in this country in the early 1800s as a ballast aboard ships. It took 79 years before it was recognized as a possible crop to be used as forage for livestock. Soy beans seemed to flourish as a crop, but it took until the 1940's before farming soy beans really took off in America. Today 55% of the world soy bean production takes place on the American continent.[1]

Soy lecithin is a by-product of soybean processing. Lecithin comes from the Greek word, lekithos, which means egg yolk. Interesting name since the color of soy lecithin resembles tiny pellets of egg yolks. The egg is considered the symbol of life, strength and fertility and some would say lecithin is also.

Lecithin is found in our own body. The brain is approximately 30% lecithin. Even our hearts have high amounts of lecithin.

It is suggested by that soy lecithin helps to lower cholesterol and I can testify to that fact.[2] If you want to do your own research on soy lecithin look for sites ending in .org. They are usually the most reliable.

You will find a delightful cracker recipe which incorporates soy lecithin along with other ingredients that have been suggested to help lower cholesterol. The delicious cracker is a part of my cholesterol lowering regime. It takes some kitchen and stove time, but the results are tasty.

A good source to purchase soy lecithin is Bob's Red Mill. This brand is reliable and available in some grocery stores and on line. It should be refrigerated to maintain freshness.

1. Ref.: http://www.soya.be/history-of-soybeans.php)
2. Ref: http://www.lecithinguide.info/soy-lecithin.html
Photos: Soy bean buds photos courtesy of ISU Extension publication, Soybean Growth and Development.
Soy bean ripe pod photo courtesy of Hopfner Werbung, Germany.

NUTRITION
SOY LECITHIN

1 Tablespoon:

		% DV*
Calories	54	
Total Fat	4 g	12%
Sat. Fat	1 g	10%
Cholesterol	0 mg	0%
Sodium	1 mg	0%
Total Carbs.	0.5 g	0%
Dietary Fiber	0 g	0%
Sugars	0.3 g	
Protein	0 g	
Calcium	10 mg	
Potassium	120 mg	

Ref: USDA website

*USDA Percent Daily Values are based on a 2,000 calorie diet. Your daily values maybe higher or lower depending on your calorie needs.

CHAPTER 6

NUTRITIONAL BREWERS YEAST

Freddy Flake

Nutritional brewers yeast, what can be said
about these golden flakes you've read
They provide the nutty flavor of delish
Along with stuff that's called nutrish

The goodness comes from where it's grown
And doctors tell us yeast is shown
To reduce the bad and bring the good
Eat your share as you should

Grab your spoon, your knife and fork
Some may even use a spork
Whatever weapon you should choose
Wash it down with a little booze

To give that booze the most effect
In the form of wine select
Not too little, not too much
Just six ounces to the touch

Nutritional Brewers Yeast

Yeast is probably older than mankind and has traveled on every path throughout the world. Yeast may be considered man's oldest industrial micro-organism. With the invention of the microscope, it became possible to isolate yeast in a pure culture form. The pioneering scientific work of Louis Pasteur in the late 1860's resulted in the ability to commercially produce baker's yeast, wine yeast, brewers yeast and nutritional yeast. Don't mistake this for live yeast that is used in making wine or beer. It is not the same. The words 'Brewers Yeast' and 'Nutritional Brewers Yeast are confusing. Hopefully, the following information will clear up any questions.

Traditionally, **Brewers Yeast** is a by-product of beer-making, which gives it a slightly bitter flavor.

Nutritional Brewers Yeast is a brewers yeast strain grown on beet molasses and cane sugar. It is a yellowish color and comes in large and small flakes or powder.

Nutritional Brewers Yeast contains the B-complex vitamins. Deficiencies of vitamins B1 (Thiamin) can lead to hand and foot numbness and possible damage to the central nervous system. Vitamin B2 (Riboflavin) deficiency may be found in vegetarians, diabetics and women taking birth control pills. B3 (Niacin) and B6 (Pyridoxine is needed for production of antibodies and red blood cells, and supports a normal functioning musculoskeletal and nervous system. People who are vegetarians and/or have compromised immune systems are most at risk of vitamin B12 deficiency. Read the label on the brand you purchase to determine the nutrition content.
Ref. wikipedia 2007.

The Brewers Yeast I found locally was bitter and difficult to work into recipes. This left me feeling very discouraged.

Pictured is my long time friend, Kate Welsh, who came to my rescue. I met Kate while volunteering at KBOO Radio. She was an engineer and I moderated a health show. Kate owned a bakery in Vermont before moving to Portland, Oregon.

Over a beer one afternoon with Kate, I was lamenting the fact that I couldn't find brewers yeast in a form that would be easy to use in cooking. She suggested using **Nutritional Brewers Yeast** and knew of a place that carried it. We downed the beer and set out for People's Co-op in Southeast Portland. It's a charming store with products not to be found elsewhere. Their Products are kept at the proper temperature and the supply is small and fresh.

Nutritional brewers yeast made by Red Star Yeast can be purchased in Portland, Oregon at People's Co-op, New Seasons, WinCo and Bob's Red Mill to name a few. Some people like it on popcorn or sprinkled on cottage cheese, stirred into yogurt or anything you can think of.

See addendum for Dr. Hassell's update on Dr. Jacobus Rinse's formula and nutrition information.

CHAPTER 7

FLAX SEED

Bright and shiny is the flax seed
Grind it into the meal you'll need
Twice as much as other ingredients
To drop your cholesterol with expedience

It gives you bulk and substance too
And helps your blood to unglue
It's taste is nutty and pretty fine
Too bad it's not as good as wine

Eat your share as you ought
To give your liver what is not
Produced as evenly as it should
So you shan't become deadwood

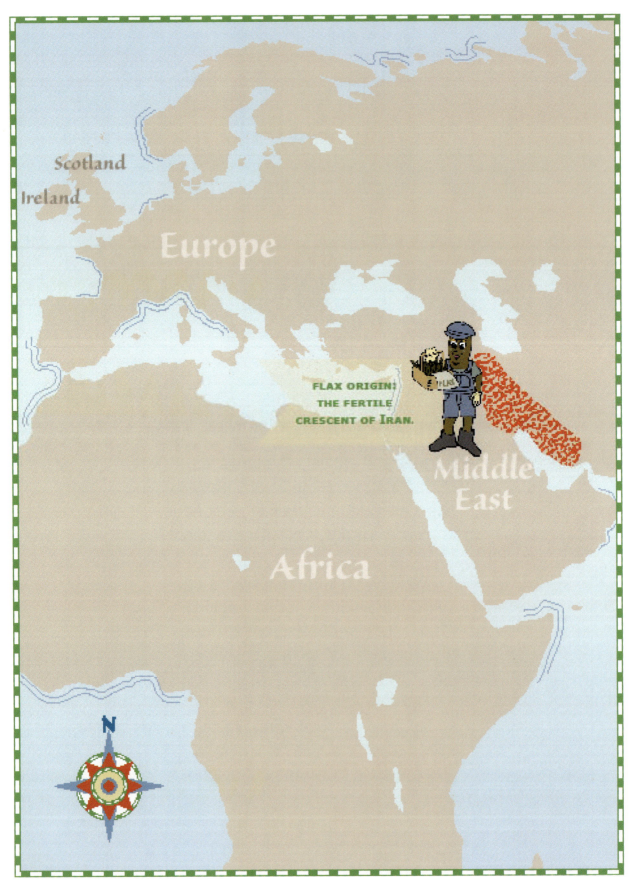

Flax Seed

About 10,000 years ago, when people began to domesticate plants for their continued survival, flax was one of the very first grains planted. Early flax cultivation is believed to have originated in what is modern day Iran. It rode on the backs of cargo carrying camels, yaks and donkeys traveling the Silk Road through China, Central Asia, and India, then on to the west and south to Iraq, Egypt, and gradually making its way around the world. As domestication progressed, the seed size increased and the oil yield became higher.

Today many varieties are grown all over the world. The seed color is brown or golden though the plants have a variety of blossom colors. Both have the same nutritional value but the golden is usually more expensive. Golden flax seed produces a lighter color product and some people think it looks more appetizing. Personally, I prefer the golden even though the nutrition is the same as the brown flax seed.

Top quality flax seed is used for cold pressed oil and seed for the human market. It is hard to believe how nutritious flax seed is. The USDA recommends that up to 12 percent flax seed can safely be used as an ingredient in food. While flax is mighty, consumption needs to be within reason.

Flax seed oil has not shown any value in lowering cholesterol. After reading this cookbook, you may become adventurous and develop your own means of using flax seed to harvest more health benefits.

Photos courtesy of North Dakota State University, Fargo, ND

Ref http://www.saskflax.com/whatisflax.html) 5-20-2008

Flax Handling and Prep

Flax seed, when left whole, holds up very well at room temperature. Once ground, it needs to be either used or covered and refrigerated to maintain integrity. Flax seed is easy enough to grind yourself in a coffee grinder, blender or food processor. I like to grind my own just before using to maintain the best quality and flavor. I've tried both the golden and brown with no difference in taste. There is a big difference in the cost though. Brown is usually less expensive and more available. Flax seed can be used whole, but it can be a little rough on the lower tract. I recommend grinding it to reap more flavor and ease of digestion.

NUTRITION

Nutrition abounds in flax seed. Its tiny size contains most of the B vitamins, magnesium, and manganese. That's just the tip of the nutrition, as flax is also rich in omega-3 fatty acids, fiber and phytochemicals including many antioxidants. Best of all, flax seed is an excellent source of lignans which tend to balance female hormones. It is also suggested lignans may help prevent type 2 diabetes and reduce cholesterol. For a full evaluation of flax seed go to the USDA website.

Ref: http://lowcarbdiets.about.com/od/whattoeat/a/flaxinfo.htm 5-20-2008

CHAPTER 8
ABOUT STUFF

About Ingredients

You don't need exotic ingredients to make food taste good. Nor is it necessary to spend a lot of time or money. Keeping the food closest to the original form of growth whether it's meat or plant based is the most nutritious and tastiest. Instead of spending your money on processed food, put it into fresh or fresh frozen food making sure it has not been processed with a lot of added calories and chemicals. Sometimes frozen vegetables are better than fresh because they have been packed quickly after picking. Also, think about how many times the product has been handled or passed through the food system to get to your mouth. Less is better.

Sweet Toothed?

If you have been cursed with a sweet tooth, you'll have a lot of work to do to get yourself reprogrammed to a diet without processed and sweetened food. You can do it though. Once you make the final slide through the keyhole, so to speak, you'll find you're not that crazy about sweets and don't feel good after eating them.

De-programming the "Sweet Tooth" is most likely easier said than done. However, you can do it the same way you get off caffeine. Just a little at a time and once in a while you'll have a relapse. Quickly forgive yourself and get back on the program to good health. You're doing it for yourself and you're the most important person you know. Like my daddy always told me, "Look out for number one!" That would be you. Don't treat your body as if it was a trash can.

Ingredient cost:

Some of these recipes call for "spendy" ingredients. If the over all cost adds flavor and brings healthful results, it's a cheap price to pay for good health. Why give your money to the giant pharmaceutical companies or food processors? Buy the best ingredients you can afford to take good care of you.

WinCo is a great store with low prices and nice quality produce. While it may not be organic, it is reasonably fresh. "Reasonably" means it should be used soon after purchasing. WinCo carries many bulk items that are less expensive and their can goods can be a bargain. New Seasons is another store that has wonderful fresh produce and they carry Bob's Red Mill products like flax seed and soy lecithin. New Seasons meat is often grown regionally. Fred Meyer has the best quality frozen okra.

Shopping:

Imagine what the size of a grocery store would be if all the processed food was removed? They would be like the old time stores from the early 1950's. There were no giant super stores then that I remember. Stores were a manageable size and easy to navigate.

It's not news that you only need to shop the perimeter of the store. The produce, meat, dairy and frozen vegetable aisles are the highlight with a few darting dashes down the paper, soap and the aisles that carry canned tomato products, beans, tea and coffee etc.

If you look down the other aisles, you see all the glittering appealing processed food. No, No, No, don't go there. They take your money, promise great things, give you coupons with money off and ruin your health as a thanks. Those aisles are packed with lies. That's how they make their money, they're like a cheap hooker hanging bling, bling things from the shelves to lure you in, quick pleasure and then do you no good. Amen!

Once in a while I'll see a coupon for money off in the produce department, but not as often as there is money off on processed food. Even the government doesn't recognize the goodness of fresh food. Please read Michael Pollan's book, "In Defense of Food." It tells the real story of food, and I highly recommend it for all who want to live a healthier life.

Cookbooks abound. High on my list is "Good Food, Great Medicine" by Mia Hassell and Dr. Miles Hassell, available on line at http://goodfoodgreatmedicine.com

If you are among the lucky ones reading this who are in excellent health, you will still enjoy the cooking methods employed. If you're reading this because your cholesterol is high and you're desperate, I believe you will love the recipes and cooking approach. It's simple to read, simple to cook, delicious to eat and very simple to clean up after.

So, please, step up to the plate! Put these little characters to work to help you enjoy new foods and better health.

Cooking Methods

Broiling

Broiling uses radiant heat from an overhead source to cook foods.

Method for broiling foods:

1. Heat the broiler.

2. Wipe the broiler grate clean with a lightly oiled towel. This will remove any particles and help season it.

3. Prepare the food to be broiled. Rub, season, or marinate it, as desired.

4. Put food in the broiler, presentation side down. If the item is oblong, place at a 45-degree angle to the bars on the grate. Cook long enough for the food to develop lines. Pull out the sliding grate and turn food over at a 90-degree angle, working from left to right.

Dry Sautéing

Dry sautéing is a dry heat cooking method that uses conduction to transfer heat from a hot sauté pan to food with the aid of a small amount of water. Foods are usually cut into small pieces and high temperatures are used in dry sautéing.

Stir-frying is a variation of sautéing. A wok is used but a frying pan can also be used. Method for Dry Sautéing Foods

1. Prepare the food to be sautéed.

2. Heat the sauté pan and add enough fat (oil or clarified butter) to just cover the pan's bottom. Heat the fat to the point where it just begins to smoke.

3. Add food to the pan, presentation side down. The food should be as dry as possible. A pan that is too large may cause the fat to burn.

4. The food should be turned and or stirred to achieve the proper color. The heat should be high enough to complete the cooking process. If the food begins to stew in its own juices continue cooking until the liquid is reduced and product browns to desired color.

5. Doneness is determined by color or touch.

Grilling

Grilling uses a heat source underneath the cooking surface.

Method for Grilling Foods:

1. Heat the grill.

2. Use a wire brush to remove any burnt particles and then season with a lightly oiled towel.

3. Prepare the food to be broiled. Rub, season, or marinate it, as desired.

4. Place food on the grill, presentation side down.

5. Turn the food to produce the crosshatch marks associated with grilling. If the item is oblong, place it at a 45-degree angle. Rotate food 90-degrees and let it cook long enough
for the grates to char it. Turn the food over and finish cooking it. You don't have to create crosshatch markings on the reverse side.

Pan-Frying

Pan-frying is similar to sautéing and deep-frying. It is a dry heat cooking method in which
heat is transferred by conduction from the pan to the food, using a moderate amount of
fat. Foods to be pan-fried are usually breaded.

Procedure For Pan-Frying Foods

1. Prepare the food. Batter or flour as desired.

2. Heat enough fat or oil to cover the item one-third to halfway up its sides. The oil should
not be as hot as used in sautéing, but should crackle. If the temperature of the oil is too
low, the food will absorb excess amounts of fat. If the temperature of the oil is too high,
the food will burn on the outside before the inside is done.

3. Add food to the pan. Always turn the food away from you to prevent being burned by
the oil. Use tongs to do this and do not pierce the food.

4. Fry the food until brown on both sides.

5. Remove the food and drain on a paper towel.

Roasting and Baking

The roasting and baking cooking methods surround the food with dry, heated air in a closed
environment. Heat is transferred by convection to the food's surface, and then penetrates
the food by conduction. The surface dehydrates, and the food browns from carmelization.

Method for Roasting or Baking Foods:

1. Preheat the oven.

2. Prepare the food. Marinate or season as desired.

3. Place the food on a rack or in a roasting pan or baking dish.

4. Roast the food, uncovered. Baste as necessary.

5. Cook to desired internal temperature keeping in mind most foods will undergo "carryover cooking". Carryover cooking occurs after a food is removed from a heat source.
This happens by the residual heat remaining in the food. (Always use a thermometer to
check the internal temperature of the item being roasted.)

Freezing Eggplant

It is so nice to have some eggplant ready to use. Take out one or two slices or several cups to prepare a dish when needed.

Buy the eggplant at a farmers market when eggplants are at the peak of freshness. Eggplants should be a creamy green color inside with a blemish free outside. There are so many varieties of eggplant and all have the same amount of nutrition. Try as many varieties as you can find to enjoy the different shapes and colors. My favorite is the typical eggplant shape with the pudgy roundness and deep purple color.

Ingredients

1   gallon water
5   500 gram vitamin C tablets*

Eggplant, peeled or not peeled, sliced in slabs, wheels, chopped or diced

* More water and vitamin C tablets should be added as needed to maintain same proportions.

2 tablespoons of vinegar can be substituted for vitamin C tablets.

Directions

1. In a large pot pour in water and bring to a boil, add the vitamin C tablets, stir to dissolve.
2. While the water is coming to a boil, prepare the eggplant. Peel or do not peel, slice in desired size pieces: Chunks, slices, wheels or slabs.
3. Place the eggplant in boiling water about 4 minutes depending on size of eggplant pieces.
4. As soon as the eggplant is *blanched, chill immediately in ice cold water. Drain, place on foil lined sheets and put in freezer.
5. When the eggplant pieces are frozen, place in zip lock bags, label, date and store in freezer.

*Blanching, also known as parboiling, is the method by which foods are partially cooked as a way to preserve their color, texture, and flavor.

Cooks Note:
Leaving skin on sometimes will cause a recipe to take on a gray color from the skins.

Freezing Eggplant
Dry Sauté Method

This method of preserving eggplant is my favorite because it uses fewer pieces of equipment and can be done without a lot of fiddle diddling. I like the added flavor from the dry sauté and the ease of using it in recipes. If your lower digestive tract allows you to eat eggplant not peeled, preparation is quicker. However, be careful, not peeling the eggplant could aggravate the business end of your lower digestive tract. Caution is the key to toleration. Another word of caution: Not peeling can add a grayish color to a dish it is used in.

Ingredients

Eggplant, washed, peeled or not peeled, cut into desired size chunks, wheels or pieces.

Directions

1. Dry sauté* , then spread the dry sautéd eggplant onto the foil lined sheet pans to cool. If your freezer is large enough, place in the freezer to cool quickly.
2. When cool enough to handle, place the amount you need for recipes into zip lock bags.
3. Press the air out of the bag and flatten for easier stacking in the freezer. Pressing flat will also help the eggplant defrost more quickly for use later.
4. Label, date and, place in the freezer.

Cooks Note: Freeze quickly, do not stack until completely frozen.
When ready to use, add to recipe as needed. It can be added frozen and is usually easier to handle if used from frozen state.

* See dry sauté method in 'About Stuff' section of cookbook.

Measure Equivalents

1 tablespoon (tbsp) =	3 teaspoons (tsp)
1/16 cup (c) =	1 tablespoon
1/8 cup =	2 tablespoons
1/6 cup =	2 tablespoons + 2 teaspoons
1/4 cup =	4 tablespoons
1/3 cup =	5 tablespoons + 1 teaspoon
3/8 cup =	6 tablespoons
1/2 cup =	8 tablespoons
2/3 cup =	10 tablespoons + 2 teaspoons
3/4 cup =	12 tablespoons
1 cup =	48 teaspoons
1 cup=	16 tablespoons
8 fluid ounces (fl oz) =	1 cup
1 pint (pt) =	2 cups
1 quart (qt) =	2 pints
4 cups =	1 quart
1 gallon (gal) =	4 quarts
16 ounces (oz) =	1 pound (lb)
1 milliliter (ml) =	1 cubic centimeter (cc)
1 inch (in) =	2.54 centimeters (cm)

Metric Conversion

Multiply	By	To Get
Fluid Ounces	29.57	grams
Ounces (dry)	28.35	grams
Grams	0.035	ounces
Grams	0.002	pounds
Kilograms	2.21	pounds
Pounds	453.6	grams
Pounds	0.454	kilograms
Quarts	0.946	liters
Quarts (dry)	67.2	cubic inches
Quarts (liquid)	57.7	cubic inches
Liters	1.057	quarts
Gallons	3785	cubic centimeters
Gallons	3.785	liters

Ref: www.nal.usda.gov/fnic/foodcomp/Bulletins/measurement_equivalents.html

Table of Equivalents

Almonds	1 pound in shell	1 1/4 cups shelled
Apples	1 pound (3 medium)	2 1/2 cups peeled and sliced
Bacon	1 pound	30 thin slices 15 thick 1 1/2 cups diced
Beans, dried	1/2 pound (1 cup)	2 1/2 cups cooked
Beans, fresh in shell	1 pound	1 cup shelled
Beets	1 pound trimmed 15 ounce can or jar	2 cups cooked and sliced 2 cups sliced
Cabbage	2 pounds	9 cups shredded or sliced 5 cups cooked
Carrots	1 pound (6-7)	3 cups sliced or shredded
Celery	1 large rib (1/4 pound)	1/2 cup sliced or chopped
Chicken	3 1/2 pounds 1 large boned breast	3 cups cooked meat 2 cups cooked meat
Chocolate	1 ounce (one square) 6 ounce package	2 tablespoons grated 1 cup morsels or chips
Cocoa	8 ounce can	2 cups
Eggplant	1 1/2 pounds	2 1/2 cups diced and cooked
Eggs, large	5 whole	1 cup
Ginger	2 inch piece	2 tablespoons grated or chopped
Herbs	1 tablespoon fresh	1 teaspoon dried
Horseradish	1 tablespoon freshly grated	2 tablespoons bottled
Lemons	1 medium	3 tablespoons juice 2 teaspoons grated rind
Limes	1 medium	1 1/2—2 tablespoons 2 teaspoons grated rind
Oats	1 cup	2 cups cooked
Okra	1 pound	5 cups
Onion	1 medium	1/2—3/4 cup chopped
Oranges	1 medium	1/3 cup juice 2—3 tablespoons grated rind
Tomatoes	1 pound (3 medium)	1 1/2 cups
Tomato paste	6 ounce can	3/4 cup

Baking Pan Equivalents

3-cup Baking Dish or Pan:

8″ x 1-1/4 round pan
10-cup Baking Dish or Pan:
8″ x 2-1/2″ springform pan
9″ x 9″ x 2″ square pan
11-3/4″ x 7-1/2″ x 1 3/4″ baking pan
13″ x 9″ x 2″ rectangular pan
15-1/2″ x 10-1/2″ x 1″ jelly-roll pan

4-cup Baking Dish or Pan:

8″ x 1-1/2″ round layer cake pan
8″ x 4″ x 2-1/2″ loaf pan
9″ x 1-1/2″ round pie pan
11″ x 1″ round tart pan

6-cup Baking Dish or Pan:

1 (8″) round cake pan
7-1/2″ x 3″ bundt tube pan
8″ x 8″ x 2″ square pan
8 1/2″ x 4-1/2″ x 2-1/2″ loaf pan
9″ x 1-1/2″ round layer cake pan
9″ x 2″ round pie plate (deep dish)
9″ x 9″ x 1-1/2″ rectangular pan
10″ x 1-1/2″ round pie plate
11″ x 7″ x 2″ rectangular pan

7-cup Baking Dish or Pan:

8″ x 2″ round cake pan
9″ x 9″ x 2″ rectangular pan

8-cup Baking Dish or Pan:

8″ x 8″ x 2″ square pan
9″ x 2″ round cake pan
9″ x 5″ x 3″ loaf pan
9″ x 9″ x 1-1/2″ square pan
9-1/4″ x 2-3/4″ ring mold
9-1/2″ x 3-1/4″ brioche pan
11″ x 7″ x 1-1/2″ baking pan

9-cup Baking Dish or Pan:

8″ x 3″ bundt pan
9″ x 3″ tube pan

11-cup Baking Dish or Pan:

9″ x 3″ springform pan
10″ x 2″ round cake pan

12-cup Baking Dish or Pan:

2 (9″) round cake pans
9″ x 3″ angel-cake pan or tube pan
10″ x 2-1/2″ springform pan
10″ x 3-1/2″ bundt pan
13″ x 9″ x 2″ metal baking pan
14″ x 10-1/2″ x 2-1/2″ roasting pan

15-cup Baking Dish or Pan:

13″ x 9″ x 2″ rectangular pan

16-cup Baking Dish or Pan:

9″ x 3-1/2″ springform pan
10″ x 4″ fancy tube mold

18-cup Baking Dish or Pan:
10″ x 4″ angel-cake or tube pan

Culinary Terms

mirepoix - (mihr-PWAH) A mixture of diced carrots, onions, celery and herbs that has been sautéed in butter or oil and used to season soups and stews. Sometimes mirepoix will contain diced prosciutto or ham to enhance flavor.

mise en place - (MEEZ ahn plahs) This technique is IMPORTANT and one that's hardest to get novice cooks to stick with. It's a French term for having all your ingredients prepped and ready to go before starting you start cooking. That means everything is cleaned, peeled, chopped, diced, measured out, whatever's necessary to get the ingredients ready prior to preparing your dish.

resting - Removing meat or poultry from heat before reaching ideal internal temperatures to allow the redistribution of juices in the meat. This helps keep the meat retain its juices, evens out temperature and doneness and easier to carve.

roux - (roo) A mixture of flour and fat that is cooked over low heat and used to thicken soups and sauces. There are three types of roux...white, blond, and brown. White and blond roux are both made with butter and used in cream sauces while brown roux can be made with either butter or the drippings from what you are cooking and is used for darker soups and sauces.

saffron - An extremely expensive yellow-orange spice made from the stigmas of purple crocus. Think about this: each crocus produces only three stigmas which are hand picked and dried. It takes 14,000 of these tiny stigmas to produce an ounce of saffron. When buying, choose the whole threads over the powder form and store in an air tight container in a cool dark place . Saffron is used for flavoring but was once used for medicinal purposes as well as dyeing clothes.

score - To make shallow cuts into the surface of foods such as fish, meat, or chicken breasts to aid in the absorption of a marinade, to help tenderize, and/or to decorate.

simmer - To cook food in liquid gently over low heat. You should see tiny bubbles just breaking the surface of the liquid.

smoking point - The point when a fat such as butter or oil smokes and lets off an acrid odor. Not good since this odor can get into what you are cooking and give it a bad flavor. Butter smokes at 350° F, vegetable oil at 445° F, lard at 365°-400°F , olive oil at about 375° F.

sweat - To cook slowly over low heat in butter, usually with the pan covered, without browning.

Worcestershire sauce - Developed in India by the British, this dark, spicy sauce got its name from the city where it was first bottled, Worcester, England. Used to season meats, gravies, and soups, the recipe includes soy sauce, onions, molasses, lime, anchovies, vinegar, garlic and tamarind, as well as other spices.

Meal Planning

So many ways to plan meals. Shoot from the hip as you tour the grocery store, have a list and stick to it, only buy things on sale... There is no best way, but writing a shopping list and taking it with you is a good start toward organization and good health. Keep a par stock of things you need.* I always keep at least two bags of frozen okra, eggplant that I froze myself, oat bran, oat groats, nutritional brewers yeast and flax seed. I like to put a date on the products when I bring them home. That makes it easier to use the FIFO method to insure freshness. FIFO stands for first in first out.

My spice drawer has over 80 spices and the necessary staples. The number and amount of things you keep on hand as your par stock depends on usage and storage space.

It's best to plan your menus in advance of shopping. I've included a sample menu to help you get started. But, you have to decide how much to eat and how many calories you can eat every day. One size does not fit all when it comes to how much to eat. It's important to eat enough food to maintain a good weight and good health. Eat proper amounts of real food rather than the processed food that pretends to be healthy.

My par stock: things like vinegar, olive oil, oat groats, oat meal, oat bran, flax seed, nutritional brewers yeast, salt and soy sauce. etc. Here is a partial list of what I keep on hand as a par stock:

*par stock is a food industry term for food on hand or pantry items you always have).

CANNED OR DRY		VEGETABLES	REFRIGERATOR
beans, any kind	oat groats	broccoli	milk, whole
beans, black	oat meal		pita bread, whole wheat
beans, garbonzo	oats, steel cut	carrots	
beans, white	olive oil	eggplant	shredded cheese
beans, pinto	salt	garlic	sharp cheddar
chicken base, Chef Mate	sardines		Stella brand three cheese
coconut milk	soy sauce	green onions	
corn, canned	sugar	lemons	tortillas, corn
diced tomatoes, canned	toasted sesame oil	limes	
flax seed	tomato paste	okra	
honey	tomato sauce	onions	
kalamata olives	tuna	pepper	
ketchup	vinegar, apple cider	spinach, fresh	
mustard, dijon	vinegar, balsamic	tomatoes, fresh	
mustard, yellow	white wine		
nutritional brewers yeast	worcestshire sauce		

SAMPLE MENU

	Breakfast	Lunch	Dinner
MON	Blueberry breakfast rinse	Potroast sandwich with cilantro cole slaw	KFC Style fried chicken Steamed broccoli
TUE	Scrambled egg w/side of breakfast branolenta 1/2 cup yogurt Fresh fruit	Sliced chicken sandwich or salad Fresh fruit	Lamb shanks Kumquat Sauce Oat groats with pomegranates
WED	Toasted beer batter bread with raspberry jam 1/2 cup plain yogurt	Sliced lamb in pita bread with sliced cabbage & yogurt	Pork leche w/apples Baked sweet potato
THU	Steel cut oatmeal with fresh berries & cream	Tuna salad in Whole wheat pita Fresh fruit	Chicken & pasta Thai style Asparagus spears
FRI	2 Eggs style of choice 2 Slices lean bacon 1 Slice whole grain toast	Broccoli salad with chicken chunks Fresh fruit	Missoula mousaka Tossed green salad w/oil & vinegar Crispy French bread
SAT	Rinse crackers w/Peanut Butter	Left over mousaka Spinach salad Whole grain bread Fresh fruit	Encrusted salmon dijon Savory dinner pudding Eggplant cake

Blueberry breakfast rinse can be eaten for any meal. It would terrific for lunch and even dinner if you're in a hurry and need a good fill-up. As you can see, it is a grand idea to prepare some extra dinner to have for lunch the next day. Just be careful not to eat it all gone at dinner. Always keep in mind portion size and control. Quality and *quantity* certainly do make a difference.

In fact, don't think of any of these meals in terms of when they should be eaten. If you dare to be different, eat dinner in the morning or maybe for lunch. There is no written rule on what foods should be eaten at certain times of the day. That's just more advertising nonsense we've been fed.

I intentionally left out the beverage on the menu. Please select a healthy beverage of your choice. Water, milk, coffee and tea work well. A glass of wine with dinner is delightful. Be sure to drink enough water during the day to stay hydrated.

CHAPTER 9
RECIPES

Let's cook!

SWEETS, SNACKS & SIDES

Blueberry Breakfast Rinse
Eggplant Spice Cake
Pineapple Express
Pecan Pudding
Beer Batter Bread
Dr J's Crackers
Broiled or Roasted Eggplant
Crispy Coconut Eggplant
Greek Salad
Asian Kid Kid
Pizza Redondo
Spunky Okra & Oat Groats
Spanish Oat Groats
Saffron Oat Groats

Blueberry Breakfast Rinse

My first adventure into eating this "rinse", named after Jacobus Rinse, was not as pleasant or as delectable as this recipe. After many different combinations, some of which would make you shiver, this recipe combines all the nutrients needed with a nice flavor burst from the blueberries. The nutty flavor of the nutritional yeast and mild crunch of the ground flax seed makes this delicious and delightful.

I like to eat this at my desk while enjoying e–news or email chatting. I follow this with my daily supplements that also help lower cholesterol, maintain good bone density, and keep my center core running like a fine machine. Chester, my doggie, waits impatiently to do the final clean up of the dish when I'm finished eating.

The two brands of yogurt I recommend are, Brown Cow and Nancy's. Each has a distinct flavor profile. Brown Cow whole milk creamy top is smooth with a full bloom of rich flavor. Nancy's brand is a little more tart. Both are equally nutritious. Give them a try and decide for yourself.

Serves 4

Ingredients

1/2 cup blueberries, fresh or frozen

1 tablespoon nutritional brewers yeast

1 tablespoon soy lecithin

2 tablespoons whole flax seed, or 4 tablespoons ground

1/2 cup plain creamy top Brown Cow yogurt

Directions

1. In microwavable container place first four ingredients.
2. Smooth yogurt on top and microwave 30 60 seconds or desired temperature. Microwave ovens vary in wattage, adjust time for your microwave. Do not overheat to avoid losing nutritional value.

Include a blueberry in every bite to enhance the eatability.

Cooks Note: The medical opinion changes regarding eating whole or ground flax seed. I prefer ground flax seed because it is easier on the digestive system. The nutrition is the same in either golden or brown colored flax seed.

If your daily calorie quota allows it, enjoy more blueberries and yogurt.

Eggplant Spice Cake

You won't believe how delicious this cake tastes. The first time I baked it I had to hide it from George because he kept sneaking pieces and Chester was his willing accomplice.

This would pack well for a road trip or lunch at your desk. Hard to believe nutrition can taste this good. If you tend to be a "sneak eater," you might want to cut this recipe in half to lessen temptation.

Serves 4

Ingredients

1 1/2	sticks butter, 6 oz
1 1/3	cups brown sugar, packed
2	teaspoons honey
4	large eggs
1 1/2	teaspoon vanilla
3/4	cup milk, whole
2	cups eggplant, peeled and shredded in the food processor
2 1/2	cups flour, all purpose
1	cups rolled oats
1/2	cup oat bran
1/2	cup nutritional brewers yeast
1/2	cup soy lecithin
1	cup ground flax seed
2	teaspoons baking powder
1	teaspoon baking soda
1	teaspoon salt
1 1/2	teaspoons cinnamon
1/2	teaspoon nutmeg
3/4	cup walnuts or pecans, optional

Tip: Sprinkle nuts on top of cake after pouring batter into pan, it makes a nice topping.

Directions

- Preheat oven
  325 degrees glass baking pan
  350 degrees metal baking pan
- Foil line or grease 9 x 13 inch pan

1. In mixer cream the butter, brown sugar and honey.
2. Add the eggs, vanilla, milk, and eggplant.
3. In separate bowl combine the dry ingredients.
4. In increments add the dry ingredients to the mixer and mix. Do not over mix.
5. Pour into foil lined or greased 9 x 13 baking pan. Bake 50 – 60 minutes. Test for doneness by inserting a knife in the center of the cake. If it comes out clean, the cake is done.

Cooks Note: Shred eggplant in food processor and pack tightly into measuring cup.

In a hurry? Pineapple Express Casserole is a truly quick fix! When you get home, before you take off your coat, turn on the oven. Then, hang up your coat and assemble the ingredients. Rinse the groats and dump everything in the baking dish.

You most likely have Corning ware. If you don't, I saw some the other day at the Salvation Army store that were really cheap. Every kitchen needs a couple of glass baking dishes and places like Salvation Army are a good source for buying them.

Back to the casserole. You'll love the ease of making this dish. But I have to tell a story on myself. The original recipe I developed called for 1/2 teaspoon pepper. I've had a jar in my spice drawer labeled telecherry pepper for years. In fact, it has moved all over the country with me. I bought it in Pennsylvania and moved it first to Chicago and then to Portland, Oregon. It never smelled like pepper, but I kept it anyway. When I started to cook this recipe, I pulled out that jar and ground it up. It still didn't smell like pepper, but being short on time I dumped it in anyway. When the recipe was baked, I tasted it. Yum, yum. Taking a bigger sniff of the ground "peppercorns", I knew it was not black pepper. It smelled delightful and familiar, but I couldn't put my finger on it.

After dinner, I jumped on the information super highway. A few key strokes later the mystery was solved when a picture of allspice popped up on my screen. Even though I'd been moving the spice around the country for 28 years, it still had a pungent aroma. I know, I know, spices are supposed to be discarded a little more often than 28 years. But, do you think the spices were all that fresh after they traveled long distances on the Silk Road?

Pineapple Express

Serve 6 – 8

Ingredients

1	cup oat groats, rinsed
1	20 ounce can pineapple tidbits or crushed in juice
1	cup water
½	tablespoon ground allspice
¼	teaspoon ground nutmeg
1	tablespoon lemon zest
1	tablespoon lime zest
½	teaspoon Sambal Oelek hot chili paste*

*Sambal Oelek brand ground fresh chili paste is available at Asian grocery stores.

Directions

- Preheat oven to 350 degrees.
  8 x 8 inch one quart glass baking dish recommended

1. Line up ingredients in order of list and place in oven proof baking dish, stir and cover.
2. Bake 50–60 minutes or until oat groats are soft. Check often to be sure it doesn't burn, add hot water if needed.

Cooks Note: The hot chili paste adds a little zip to the dish. This could be a fab dessert too!.

Nutty Pudding - sweet or savory

For those seeking quick fixing food, this dish takes a few flicks of the wrist. Brunch, lunch or supper would be complemented by this recipe. If this were in a wine magazine it would be described as follows:

Juicy raisins clamoring for attention while pecans sneak in behind with a vibrant crunch reminiscent of a rich dessert while holding court with nutrition. The sweet notes of orange peel reflect the flavor of old fashioned rice pudding with the new quality of brilliant vitamins and minerals.

The name oat groats some how doesn't resonate the same as rice in recipes, however the power packed punch of vitamins makes up for the lack of beauty in the name. Dauntingly delicious!

Serves 4

Ingredients

2/3 cup oat groats, rinsed
1 ⅓ cups water

3   large eggs
2   cups milk
½   cup sugar
½   cup raisins
½   cup toasted pecans, or cashews*
½   tablespoon grated orange peel
¼   teaspoon salt
¼   teaspoon ground nutmeg

Garnish with cinnamon and chopped nuts.

Directions

- Preheat oven to 350 degrees for metal pan, 325 degrees for glass dish.
- Foil line baking pan for easy clean up

1. Heat the water in medium sauce pan. Add the oat groats and simmer about 20 minutes. Drain and cool.
2. In large bowl whisk the eggs. Stir in the milk, sugar, raisins, pecans, orange peel, and salt.
3. Add the cooled oat groats to egg mixture and combine. Pour into baking dish and sprinkle nutmeg over top. Bake uncovered 50–60 minutes. Serve warm

Serving suggestions: Side dish for chicken or pork; or dessert with a little cinnamon sprinkled on top.

Cooks Note: Oat groats must be cool or the eggs will cook when added.
*Pecans may work a little better than cashews.

Beer Batter Bread

This is another opportunity to enjoy a daily dose of nutritional brewers yeast, oat bran, ground flax seed and soy lecithin all wrapped in a beer flavor. I've tried this with water instead of beer and it works well. However, I found myself longing to dip it in a glass of suds to give it that missing tang.

I like this toasted and smeared with raspberry chipotle jam. Chester, my doggie, sits at attention waiting for meager crumbs. Be careful of giving too much of this tasty cuisine to canines as they have a little trouble digesting it and doggie toots are troublesome.

Serves 4

Ingredients

3 cups brown rice **flour**
2 tablespoons baking powder
6 tablespoons sugar
2 teaspoons salt
2 cups ground flax seed
1 cup brewers yeast
1 cup soy lecithin
1 cup oat bran

1/3 cup kalamata olives, slilced in half (more or less olives as desired)
1 6 ounce container feta cheese crumbles
3 cups beer or water (beer gives more robust flavor, but adds calories)
3 tablespoons butter, melted
2 tablespoons garlic, smashed & chopped

Directions

1. Cover sheet pan with foil. I use a commercial size half pan 13 x 18, well worth purchasing. Preheat oven: 375 degrees
2. In large bowl place dry ingredients and thoroughly mix. This is important to be sure the *Rinse* mixture is evenly distributed. (See index for Rinse formula)
3. Add the kalamata olives and feta cheese, mix to coat with dry ingredients.
4. Make a well in center of dry ingredients, add the beer and mix by hand, being careful not to over mix.
5. Pour batter onto sheet pan and spread evenly, sprinkle garlic over the top and drizzle with melted butter. Bake 50–60 minutes or until an inserted knife point comes out clean. Cool, cut into 12 pieces.

Dr J's Crackers

You'll enjoy these crackers for many reasons. The added crunch is a nice addition to getting and keeping your cholesterol down. They're great for a meal with a bit of peanut butter on top or served with a favorite soup.

This recipe is a snap to make. Use a tortilla press to speed the process. If you have a large heavy duty food processor this recipe can be increased by 6. See ingredient list on next page.

1 Days Serving - 6 crackers

Ingredients

1½ cups rolled oats
3   rounded tablespoons soy lecithin
3   rounded tablespoons brewers yeast
¾   cups ground flax seed
½   teaspoon salt
½   cup water
Heavy duty plastic sandwich bag

Toppings: Sesame or poppy seeds, chopped nuts, or dried fruit.

Directions

- Food processor
- Preheat oven to 375 degrees
- 1 sheet of heavy duty aluminum foil large enough to hold each days portion about 18" x 22"

1. In food processor using the steel knife blade place all the dry ingredients.
2. Pulse the processor on and off to mix the dry ingredients.
3. With food processor motor running pour in a steady stream of water. Process another 10 seconds. Dough should have formed a large ball. If dough feels dry, add water one teaspoon at a time, process until ball forms. Be careful not to over process. You may have to add water and mix by hand to avoid over processing.
4. When the dough has formed a ball, remove from the processor. Knead the dough for 30 seconds. Cover with plastic or put in zip lock bag, let rest 30 minutes. Can be left in cool place overnight. Dough rolls out better when it's at room temperature.
5. Slice dough into six equal pieces.

Directions continued on next page.

Dr. J's Crackers, con't

Rolling Crackers

1. Slit the heavy duty plastic sandwich bag on two sides. Open the tortilla press, place the bag in the center of the press and open the bag. Then, place the dough ball in the center of one half of the plastic bag. Fold the other half of the plastic bag over the top of the dough ball. Gently close the press and press down until the dough has spread to desired thickness.
2. Open the tortilla press, peel back the plastic bag, then sprinkle on topping of choice and press again. If needed, moisten with a little water before adding topping to make topping stick better.
3. The pressed cracker will be wheel shaped. Using a knife, score or cut lines in the dough to form pie shaped pieces. Do not cut all the way through dough. Place formed cracker on aluminum foil sheet. Repeat until all dough is used with six crackers per foil sheet.
4. Carefully place the foil with the crackers into the oven. Bake 15 - 18 minutes depending on thickness of cracker or until cracker begins to brown.

Baking tips:
– *When the crackers are baked, leave the crackers on the foil sheets and put back in the oven. TURN OFF OVEN! Leave the crackers in oven to completely dry out and crisp up until oven cools. Can be left over night.*
– *Stack the crackers on top of each other and wrap in the same aluminum foil used for baking.*
– *Store in cool dry place. If stored in plastic bag, crispness could be lost.*
– *Crackers can be frozen for up to three months.*

If you have a large heavy duty food processor, this recipe can used:

Yield: 6 day cracker supply
3   cups rolled oats
6   rounded tablespoons soy lecithin
6   rounded tablespoons nutritional
       brewers yeast
1 1/2 cups ground flax seed
1   teaspoon salt
1   cup water

Broiled or Roasted Eggplant

The simplicity of roasting or broiling eggplant demands your attention. Keeping some prepared and frozen can add a delightful flavor to various dishes and a health benefit also. Take care not to dry them out when cooking. If you get them too dry don't despair. You can always use them in soups or sauces. If by chance you turn them into a cinder, well, try again. Don't give up on this delicious addition to your food world.

Need a snack? Broiled or roasted eggplant is the ticket when you want to watch your calories but need a little boost during the day.

I must work on an ice cream recipe that includes eggplant, it sure works well in brownies and other sweet things. Eggplant takes on the flavor of most dishes and is an underrated member of the veggie clan.

Serves 4

Ingredients

1   eggplant, any size desired
• olive oil

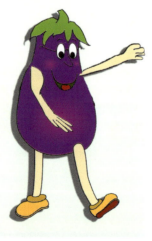

Directions

• Preheat oven to 350 degrees / or turn on broiler.

1. Peel or don't peel the eggplant. Slice in desired size, place on foil lined sheet pan, brush with olive oil. Turn after baking about 10 minutes, bake another 10 minutes or until tender— about 20 minutes for half inch thick slices. Adjust the baking time for thickness of eggplant slices.

Cooks Note: If broiling turn often and cook until tender. Watch carefully so it doesn't burn.

Crispy Coconut Eggplant

Crispy coconut eggplant could be used as a scrumptious snack or appetizer. It would go well with a glass of wine or cup of tea. Serve a dipping sauce of chocolate to bring out evocative scents of a Mounds candy bar. Mmmm, take another bite and enjoy a luscious way to help lower your cholesterol.

Chester gave this a paws up. He enjoyed cleaning out the measuring cup that held the beer. Doggies shouldn't drink beer, but a tiny drop once in a while sure makes him happy.

Serves 4

Ingredients:

1 medium eggplant, peeled or unpeeled, ½ inch slices

First coating mixture:
1 2 large eggs
½ cup cornstarch
1 cup beer
1½ teaspoon baking powder

Second coating mixture:
2 cups unsweetened flaked coconut
½ cup oat bran

3 tablespoons toasted sesame oil

Directions:

- Preheat oven to 425 degrees
- Foil line sheet pan

1. In medium bowl combine the egg, cornstarch, beer and baking powder.
2. In shallow pan or plate combine the coconut and oat bran.
3. Dip eggplant first into the egg coating mixture and then into the coconut mixture. Place on sheet pan. Drizzle sesame oil over the top of the eggplant. Bake 20 minutes or until tender. Baking time depends on the thickness of the eggplant slices.

Cooks Note: If these brown too fast without cooking, reduce the oven temperature.

I can't emphasize the need to fully COOK eggplant enough. It must always be cooked.

This Greek salad is a somewhat shy reserved addition to a meal of rack of lamb or it can be an outrageous stand alone entree. The apple adds a nice crunch with a pleasant sour note. Serve an orange colored vegetable such as acorn or butternut squash in the fall or winter and maybe cooked carrots in the spring to brighten the meal.

George rated this 5 stars, while Chester had to sit this one out because the recipe has onions and onions are not good for doggies.

Don't forget, even though this is a salad, quantity control needs to be exercised. The calorie count of cheese and olives adds up quickly.

Serves 2

Greek Salad

Ingredients

¼ medium eggplant, peeled and sliced into ½ inch thick x 2 inch pieces
½ red pepper, diced
¼ onion, finely chopped
¼ cup kalamata olives sliced in half
½ Granny Smith apple, cut in quarters and sliced thin
½ cup feta cheese, crumbled

Dressing:
1 tablespoon dijon mustard
3 tablespoons olive oil
2 tablespoons honey
2 tablespoons balsamic or apple cider vinegar
¼ teaspoon white pepper or to taste

Directions

1. In a saucepan place the eggplant and cover with about a half inch of water. Bring to boil reduce heat and simmer about 10 minutes or until tender. Chill quickly in cold water, drain thoroughly.
2. When the eggplant is cooled and drained, place in a large bowl. Add the red pepper, onion, olives, apple and cheese.

Dressing:
1. In a bowl whisk together mustard, olive oil, vinegar, honey and pepper.
2. Pour the dressing over the eggplant and apple mixture and gently toss.

To serve, have ready chilled plates. Arrange salad on plate, garnish with a few pieces of diced red pepper.

Branolenta is a combination of words: Oat bran and polenta. As you may know, polenta is made from corn meal and is a popular side dish in Italian cooking. I borrowed the "lenta" from polenta even though there is no corn meal in the recipe. Branolenta can easily be substituted for polenta.

Corn meal doesn't pack much of a nutrition punch compared to oat bran. Oat bran is a very important part of helping to lower cholesterol. What better way to eat oat bran than to dress it up and use it instead of polenta, potatoes, noodles or rice?

I keep a batch made up frozen and wrapped in individual packages to have on hand when needed. Sometimes I use it for a "crust" in casseroles. Herbs and spices can be added to enhance the flavor making it sweet or savory. Branolenta in any meal gives you a high grade nutrition blast.

Basic Branolenta

4 ½ cup Servings

Ingredients

3   cups water
½   teaspoon salt (optional)
¼   teaspoon white pepper
1   cup oat bran

Directions

1. In a large sauce pan heat the water. Stir in salt, pepper and oat bran. Bring to boil, reduce heat and simmer about 5 minutes.
2. Serve as is, or pour the polenta into 8 by 8-inch cake pan lined with parchment paper or foil. Place in the refrigerator to cool completely.

Once set, turn the polenta out onto a cutting board and cut into squares, rounds, or triangles. Brush each side with olive oil and sauté in a nonstick skillet over medium heat, or grill.

Fried Branolenta

4 ½ cup Servings

Ingredients

1   recipe basic Branolenta cut in desired size slices
2   tablespoons olive oil

Directions

1. Heat medium size (teflon) skillet, add olive oil. Place slices of branolenta in heated olive oil and brown about 5 – 8 minutes on each side.

Cooks Note: Add more oil if needed when frying.

Basic Oat Groats

4½ cup Servings

Ingredients

2   cups water
1   cup oat groats, rinsed in colander or strainer
½   teaspoon salt optional

Directions

1. Heat the water in a large sauce pan, add the oat groats. Bring to a boil, simmer 20—30 minutes or until tender but not mushy.

Cooks Note: A pinch of salt is optional, but certainly not necessary. Oat groats are delightful at any meal including breakfast.

Asian Kid Kid

Pairing kidkid with a sweet chili dipping sauce makes this recipe stellar, absolutely stellar! The taste is a subtle combination of flavors with nutty notes and just a bit of a zing at the end. Served as an appetizer, part of the main course, or even a quick breakfast makes it a winner. I serve a dipping sauce with it called "Mae Ploy Sweet Chilli Sauce" which is available at Asian grocery stores. A little hot mustard or even ketchup for a dipper would give this a glorious taste sensation.

What a wonderful way to include the whole oat groat in your meals. Oat groats are underrated and underused as a wonderful source of vitamins and minerals. In fact, they have more nutrition to offer than brown rice.

Yield: Approximately 36 balls

Ingredients:

2   cups water
1   cup oat groats, rinsed

¼   cup minced onion
2   tablespoons Kikoman soy sauce
3   large eggs
¼   cup oat bran (add more if needed to make balls stick together)
½   teaspoon black pepper
½   teaspoon granulated garlic powder
1   teaspoon Sambal Oelek* brand ground fresh chili paste (optional)

Coating:
1½ cups Stella brand shredded 3 Cheese Italian blend
¾   cup oat bran

*Sambal Oelek brand ground fresh chili paste is available at Asian grocery stores or on line.

Sauce pictured is Mae Ploy brand sweet chili sauce. Sweet/sour sauce of your choice can be used.

Directions:

- Preheat oven to 425 degrees
- Line sheet pan with foil then rub lightly with olive oil
1. Heat the water in a large sauce pan. Add the rinsed oat groats, bring to a boil, reduce heat to a simmer, then cover and cook about 20–30 minutes or until tender. Drain in colander or strainer and cool enough to handle by running cold water over them. When cool, drain thoroughly.
2. In a large bowl combine the cooled oat groats, onion, soy sauce, eggs, oat bran, pepper, garlic powder, and chili paste.
3. In a separate shallow pan combine the coating mixture of cheese and oat bran.
4. Drop teaspoons of oat groat mixture into coating, roll into a ball covering ball with the coating and place on a sheet pan close together. Bake at 425 degrees 20 minutes or until golden.

Serve with dipping sauce.

Cooks Note: If balls won't hold together, add more oat bran until ball forms and sticks together.

Pizza Redondo

Hors d'oeuvres for children or adults. You can't go wrong with these for a scrumptious treat. I fell into this recipe when I was teaching a cooking class to 11–13 year olds at a community center. I wanted to introduce them to healthy foods but knew it had to relate to their age and taste buds. I was a little nervous about presenting this recipe. Haha on me! It was a big hit. They made sure to save some to take home. After class I saw them telling the front desk people about the pizza redondos.

This recipe goes to the front of the list for dishes to take to gatherings. It can be a meal accompaniment or a main dish, great for the lunch bucket or terrific packed for a road trip.

Yield: Approximately 36 Redondos

Ingredients:

2	cups water
1	cup oat groats, rinsed
1	cup shredded cheddar cheese
¼	cup minced onion
3	large eggs
½	can tomato paste
¼	cup oat bran
½	teaspoon black pepper
½	teaspoon granulated garlic powder
1	tablespoon oregano

Coating:
2	cups shredded Tillamook mozzarella cheese
¾	cup oat bran

Sauce:

1	tablespoon olive oil
½	can tomato paste (use other half of can)
1	tablespoon oregano or to taste
½	can water (use empty tomato paste can)

1. In a small sauce pan heat the olive oil. Add the tomato paste, sauté briefly.
2. Add the oregano, stir in the water and cook until bubbly.

Serve in small bowl and use as a dipping sauce

Directions:

- Preheat oven to 425 degrees
- Line sheet pan with foil then rub lightly with olive oil

1. Heat the water in a large sauce pan. Add the rinsed oat groats, bring to a boil, reduce heat to a simmer, then cover and cook about 20–30 minutes or until tender. Drain in colander or strainer and cool enough to handle by running cold water over them. When cool, drain and set aside.
2. In a large bowl combine the cooled oat groats, cheddar cheese, onion, eggs, oat bran, pepper, garlic powder, and oregano.
3. Drop a rounded teaspoon (or more depending on size ball desired) of the mixture into the coating, toss coating mixture over the top, pick up and roll into a ball, place on a sheet pan close together (they don't spread). Bake at 425 degrees 30–40 minutes until golden.

Serve with dipping sauce.

Spunky Okra & Oat Groats

Two very, very lean pieces of bacon will not a diet ruin. Besides, these aren't diet recipes, they're ways to eat better to control your cholesterol. Eating bacon, very lean bacon and very small amounts, brings a nice flavor profile to this dish.

Serve this as a side dish with any meal or maybe as a breakfast adventure. Breakfast doesn't have to be what the advertising industry is selling.

You can begin or end your day with this wallop of nutrition. It doesn't take a lot of time or resources to eat well and take care of yourself. No matter how often you think it's a waste of time, it certainly isn't! Step out into your day with these exciting nutrients under your belt. You're worth the bother, aren't you?

Serves 4

Ingredients

2	slices lean bacon, fat trimmed, chopped
1	medium onion, chopped
4	cloves garlic, minced
1	cup okra, frozen cut
1	15 ounce can diced tomatoes with liquid
1	teaspoon ground thyme
1	cup oat groats, rinsed
2	cups water
1	rounded teaspoon chicken base **or** ½ teaspoon salt
2	tablespoons Bubbies Horseradish* or to taste

*Bubbies Horseradish is naturally brined. www.bubbies.com

Directions

1. Heat skillet, dry sauté the bacon until crispy, drain the grease if there is any. Add the onions and dry sauté'.
2. Add the garlic, okra, tomatoes, thyme, oat groats and water. Stir in the chicken base, then bring to a boil, reduce heat, cover and simmer 25–30 minutes or until the oat groats are tender. Add more water if needed. Taste and adjust seasonings.

Serve as side dish for chicken or steak.

Cooks Note: Leftovers could be used in soup or reheated for another meal.
Bubbies Horseradish is available at New Seasons Market in Portland, OR.

Spanish Oat Groats

If you enjoy rich, deeply flavorful food, put this recipe at the top of your list. Oat groats lend themselves to nearly any flavor profile and their ease of cooking and nutritional value should encourage you to try include them in your dining as much as possible.

This recipe is a delicious accompaniment to steak, chicken, and Mexican entrees such as tacos or enchiladas. It can also be served as a breakfast side dish in place of hash browns. Put a bottle of hot sauce on the table for those who enjoy a bigger blast of heat.

Serves 4

Ingredients

1	medium onion, chopped
1	cup water
2	cans 14.5 ounce tomatoes, fire roasted
1	medium green pepper, chopped
¾	cup oat groats, rinsed
1	tablespoon brown sugar
1	tablespoon Lea & Perrins Worcestershire sauce
1	teaspoon chili powder, mild or hot
¼	teaspoon Red Devil hot sauce (optional)

Directions

1. Heat skillet, dry sauté the onion until golden brown.
2. Add the remaining ingredients and simmer 30–40 minutes or until the oat groats are tender.

Serving suggestions: As a tasty side dish to perk up a meal or that perfect side with scrambled eggs.

Cooks Note: Recipe would be delightful frozen in individual portions to be used later.

Saffron Oat Groats

The flavor and fragrance of saffron is released only by cooking in hot water based liquid. The exotic touch will be lost if cooked in oil. It's difficult to find a good source for saffron, but worth the trouble as it has a lovely subtle flavor.

Oat groats lend themselves to nearly any dish requiring rice. The nutty flavor and texture will give a recipe traction and make you want to dig right in. One cup each of okra and eggplant can be bundled with the bright green peas and carrots for an added nutrition thrust. It's scrumptious included in a meal of beef, chicken or pork.

Don't forget it would be a tasty breakfast, pack it for lunch or a quick energy lift in the afternoon.

Serves 4

Ingredients

¼   teaspoon whole cumin seeds
½   cup onion, chopped
½   cup carrots, sliced or diced
3   cups water
20 saffron threads*
3   whole cloves
1   stick whole cinnamon

1   teaspoon chicken base **or** ½ teaspoon salt
1   cup oat groats, rinsed

½   cup peas, frozen

*use more or less saffron to desired taste.

Directions

1. Heat a large skillet and dry sauté the onions until golden colored.
2. Add the water, saffron, cloves, cinnamon, cumin seeds, chicken base, and oat groats. Stir and bring to boil, reduce heat to simmer, cover and cook 20—25 minutes or until the oat groats are tender.
3. Stir in the peas and add water if necessary to keep from drying out. Continue cooking until the peas are heated through about 5 minutes

Serve with beef, chicken or pork.

Cooks Note: Cooking the peas only until heated through will help retain their attractive bright green color.

Marinated Vegetables
- **Asian**
- **Curried**
- **Mediterranean**
- **Mexican**

Marinated Roasted Vegetables
Asian Style

When I was a kid, my first experience with soy sauce was at a Chinese restaurant called Ding Ho's in Waukegan, Illinois. A full lunch was 40¢ which included the most delicious soft roll. Once in a while on payday, my mother would take us shopping and out for lunch at Ding Ho's. Mother would greet the owner by saying "Hello, Mrs. Ho." Mrs. Ho would burst into giggles and run into the kitchen. I wish I knew what Ding Ho meant. I'm pretty sure it wasn't her name.

This recipe has a lovely dark mahogany shade of brown with a scrumptious flavor. Added to dishes or used as a condiment alone is a tasty treat. The peppers contribute potassium along with the cholesterol lowering eggplant and okra.

Yield: 6 cups

Ingredients:

Marinade:
1   cup toasted sesame oil
¼   cup Kikoman soy sauce
1   tablespoon ginger powder
4   teaspoons garlic, minced
1   tablespoon Chinese five spice
1   tablespoon ketchup
¼   cup honey

Vegetables:
2   cups okra, frozen cut
2   cups eggplant, (2 cups) cut in ½ inch thick slices, peeled or not peeled
1   medium onion cut in one inch square pieces
1   each: red pepper, green pepper, cut in one inch pieces

Tip: Veggies should be cut the same size and thickness to cook evenly.

Directions:

- Preheat oven to 425 degrees
- Foil line baking pan for easy clean up

1. Place all the marinade ingredients into a 2.5 gallon resealable plastic bag, close and squeeze bag to mix.
2. To the bag add the okra, eggplant, onion and peppers. Manipulate bag to mix all ingredients. Marinate two hours or overnight in the refrigerator.
3. Drain the vegetables and spread evenly on a sheet pan. Bake 15 minutes, turn the vegetables and bake another 15 minutes or until the vegetables are tender. Take care not to burn.

Cooks Note: The flavor is based on Kikoman soy sauce, other soy sauces can be used but be careful of their saltiness.

Make into a divine veggie spread or spike up a salad.

The eggplant measurement is approximate, if you have more eggplant go ahead and use it.

This recipe freezes well. Freeze in one cup portions to use in other recipes.

Marinated Roasted Vegetables
Curry Style

When I was 20 and just married, my next door neighbors were my first introduction to exotic food and flavors. Andre was a world traveler who used spices beyond the salt and pepper I grew up with. Andre was a master at curried rice and taught me the nuances of using curry.

My children grew up with Sunday night supper consisting of chicken and curried rice. To this day, my kids smell curried rice and fondly remember "Sunday night supper" when we gathered around the TV to eat and watch 60 Minutes. Wonderful memories with tick, tick, tick as the show intro said to my family, "Dinner is served."

With curry on these veggies, consider lamb, pork or chicken dishes. Maybe toss in some raisins, dried cranberries, chopped dates or prunes to add sweetness and texture.

Yield: 6 cups

Ingredients

Marinade:

1	cup sesame oil
1	cup apple cider vinegar
¼	cup lemon juice
1	tablespoon mild curry powder
4	cloves garlic, chopped (4 tablespoons)

Vegetables:

2	cups okra, frozen cut
12	ounces eggplant (2 cups), cut in ½ inch thick slices, peeled or not peeled
1	medium onion cut in one inch square pieces
1	each: red pepper, green pepper, and yellow pepper cut in one inch square pieces or any combination of peppers

Tip: Veggies should be cut the same size and thickness to cook evenly.

Directions

- Preheat oven to 425 degrees
- Foil line baking pan for easy clean up

1. Place all the marinade ingredients into a 2.5 gallon resealable plastic bag, close and squeeze bag to mix.
2. To the bag add the okra, eggplant, onion and peppers. Manipulate bag to mix all ingredients. Marinate two hours or overnight in the refrigerator.
3. Drain the vegetables and spread evenly on a sheet pan. Bake 15 minutes, turn the vegetables and bake another 15 minutes or until the vegetables are tender. Take care not to burn.

Serving suggestions: Goes well with beef, lamb or chicken. Delightful stuffed in pita pocket or part of a salad.

Cooks Note: The eggplant measurement is approximate, if you have more eggplant go ahead and use it.

This recipe freezes well. Freeze in one cup portions to use in other recipes.

Marinated Roasted Vegetables
Mediterranean Style

The intriguing blend of these vegetables, herbs and spices in this recipe represent a large part of the food and culture around the Mediterranean Sea. The term "Mediterranean" can mean North African (especially Morocco), eastern Mediterranean (Egypt, Greece, Israel, Lebanon, Syria and Turkey), and southern Europe (Italy, France, and Spain) or simply put, any country that touches the Mediterranean Sea.

This delectable recipe can be added to spaghetti sauce or tossed with plain cooked pasta, rice or oat groats. It could enhance pizza or stand alone with cheese mixed in or spread on top of pita bread and eaten cold or heated. I like to make it and freeze it in small amounts.

George found some in the freezer, ate it and said, "I don't know what it was, but it sure was good." Lucky I had it labeled so I could look at the empty bag to see what he ate.

Yield: 6 cups

Ingredients

Marinade:
1   cup olive oil
1   cup dry white wine
6   tablespoons lemon juice
4   cloves garlic, minced
1   teaspoon salt
½   teaspoon pepper or to taste
1   teaspoon thyme

Vegetables:
2   cups okra, frozen cut
12   ounces (2 cups) eggplant cut in 2 inch x ½ inch pieces
1   medium onion, cut in 1 inch square pieces
1   each: red pepper, green pepper, and yellow pepper cut in one inch square pieces or any combination of peppers

Tip: Veggies should be cut the same size and thickness to cook evenly.

Directions

- Preheat oven to 425 degrees
- Foil line baking pan for easy clean up

1. Place all the marinade ingredients into a large resealable plastic bag, close and squeeze bag to mix.
2. To the bag add the okra, eggplant, onion and peppers. Manipulate bag to mix all ingredients. Marinate two hours or overnight in the refrigerator.
3. Drain the vegetables and spread evenly on a sheet pan. Bake 15 minutes, turn the vegetables and bake another 15 minutes or until the vegetables are tender. Take care not to burn.

Serving suggestions: Pizza topping, side dish for chicken or lamb. Heavenly used on gyro or over branolenta slices (see index for recipe). This recipe is used in the White Tie Pasta recipe (see index)

Cooks Note. This recipe freezes well. Freeze in one cup portions to use in other recipes.

The eggplant measurement is approximate, if you have more eggplant go ahead and use it.

2.5 gallon resealable bags are available at some grocery stores.

Marinated Roasted Vegetables
Mexican Style

Tortillas make a delicious platform for marinated roasted vegetables. Slather on a layer of guacamole, add some sliced cabbage and Mexican roasted veggies to help complete the cholesterol lowering foods with a flourish.

Tossing some roasted veggies into a chopped cabbage for a salad or adding it to an omelette will entice everyone to eat.

A whiff of this recipe brings images of walking through a small Mexican town, street vendors hawking their wares, shy children peeking out from behind their mother's skirt and guitars strumming La Cucaracha...

Yield: 6 cups

Ingredients

Marinade:
1 cup olive oil
½ cup tequila
1/3 cup lime juice
3 teaspoons garlic, minced
1 tablespoon cumin
1 cup cilantro leaves
1 tablespoon chili powder, mild
1 teaspoon salt

Vegetables:
2 cup okra, frozen cut
12 ounces eggplant (2 cups) cut in 2 inch x ½ inch pieces, peeled or not peeled
1 medium onion, cut in 1 inch square pieces
1 green or red pepper cut in 1 inch pieces

Tip: Veggies should be cut the same size and thickness to cook evenly.

Directions

- Preheat oven to 425 degrees
- Foil line baking pan for easy clean up

1. Place all the marinade ingredients into a large resealable plastic bag or large container, close and squeeze bag to mix.
2. To the bag add the okra, eggplant, onion and peppers. Manipulate bag to mix all ingredients. Marinate two hours or overnight in the refrigerator.
3. Drain the vegetables and spread evenly on a sheet pan. Bake 15 minutes, turn the vegetables and bake another 15 minutes or until the vegetables are tender. Take care not to burn.

Serving suggestions: Add to tacos or enjoy over rice.

Cooks Note. This recipe freezes well. Freeze in one cup portions to use in other recipes.

The eggplant measurement is approximate, if you have more eggplant go ahead and use it.

2.5 gallon resealable bags are available at some grocery stores.

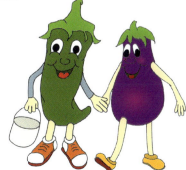

83

BEEF

Greek Tortillas
Creamed Hamburger
Brandy Beef Pot Roast
Missoula Mousaka
Beef Stroganoff
Beef Mediterranean Wraps
Tex-Mex Bake
Beef Chardonnay
Mustard Beef Short Ribs
Beef – Lamb Gyro

Greek Tortilla

I don't get back to the Chicago area very often, but when I do, the one stop I love to make is a small falafel shop in Skokie, Illinois. I'll never forget the time my daughter picked me up at the airport and we decided a falafel stop was needed. My granddaughter, Syniva, was two at the time and I mean really two. The minute we hit the door of the shop, she started acting up as only a two year old can do. In between spilled pop, intermittent high pitched yips and loud "NO, I don't want to's" we managed to have a sandwich similar to this one. The sandwich was divine in spite of Syniva's antics.

It's hard to eat only one of these flop-overs. The crunch of the cabbage adds a rhythm to chewing pleasure while delivering nutrients to our diet. It could be called a feast in your fist.

Serves 4

Ingredients:

1	pound ground beef
1	tablespoon ground chipotle pepper
1	tablespoon mild chili powder
¼	cup water
1	container of purchased black bean dip (optional) or 2 tablespoons cooked black beans sprinkled on each tortilla
2	cups thinly sliced cabbage
2	tomatoes, diced
1	recipe Mediterranean marinated veggies (see recipe index)
4	whole wheat 10 inch flour tortillas or whole grain pita bread

Directions:

1. Heat a large skillet. Add the beef stirring until brown. Pour off the grease.
2. Stir in the chipotle pepper, chili powder and water, cook about 5 minutes on low heat to marry flavors.

To assemble sandwich:
1. Lightly grill the tortillas on directly on stove burner, flipping often until toasted. Set aside and keep warm or toast in skillet.
2. Spread the black bean dip evenly over the warm toasted tortilla or sprinkle cooked beans.
3. Place the ground beef mixture on top of the bean dip, cover with the cabbage and sprinkle tomatoes on top. Flop in half and serve.

Cooks Note: Toasting tortillas or pita bread directly on stove burner is quick and easy. Be careful not burn as they toast quickly.

86

Creamed Hamburger

Creamed hamburger is an old standby dressed up and delivered in a new way. I don't know why oat bran is not used more. It thickens recipes by adding a nutty flavor and fiber while being every bit as easy to use as flour.

This was a family favorite my Daddy used to make on Sunday mornings after church. He called it S.O.S. We'd ask what that meant and he'd just laugh. Daddy never used bad language and insisted people needed to speak proper English or not speak at all. He was a sailor in the navy and a soldier in the army. He told us that S.O.S. was served in both branches of the service.

I was at a friend's house and they served creamed beef and I said it was S.O.S. not creamed beef. That statement was met with a stunned silence around the table. I went home and told my Mother the story. Through sputters and gulps of laughter she told me the real meaning of S.O.S. No wonder they were shocked, so was I - at my Dad.

Serves 4

Ingredients

1   pound ground beef, 10 % fat
1   cup medium onion, chopped
1   medium green pepper, chopped
1   teaspoon chicken base (see index) **or** ½ teaspoon salt
¼   cup oat bran
2   cups whole milk
½   cup frozen green peas

Chopped parsley for garnish (optional)

Directions

1. Heat a large skillet and brown the ground beef. Add the onion and cook until the onion is transparent. Drain grease.
2. Add the green pepper, stir in the chicken base.
3. Sprinkle the oat bran over the top and stir.
4. Slowly stir in the milk and bring to a simmer. Cook 5 minutes or until thickened. Add the green peas stirring until peas are heated through.

To serve, have ready warmed plates. If serving the creamed hamburger over oat groats, arrange some oat groats in the center of each plate. Spoon creamed beef over the top of the oat groats. Garnish with chopped parsley and serve immediately.

Serving suggestions: serve over cooked oat groats, branolenta (see index), potatoes, brown rice or toast.
Soup could be made by thinning with milk or water and adding vegetables.

Missoula Mousaka

When my kids were young in the 70s, we traveled to Missoula, Montana to visit relatives. We went to "the" new Greek restaurant run by two brothers, the name of which I've long forgotten. They were serving mousaka, a very exotic foreign dish to me at the time. This recipe is the result.

Until I went to cooking school, I thought mousaka was a tomato based dish. I even argued with the instructor at the Culinary Institute of America. He asked me where I got this idea. I told him about my experience with Greek cuisine in Missoula, Montana. He had tears running down his face with laughter, "Dahlink, I doubt a place named Missoula would really know Greek cooking."

Serves 4–6

Ingredients

1   cup oat groats, rinsed
2   cups water

Olive oil
1   pound ground beef
2   cups chopped onions
1   medium green pepper, chopped
4   cloves garlic, minced
2   cups okra, cut frozen
2   teaspoons oregano
2   teaspoons basil
2   14.5 ounce cans crushed tomatoes
1   teaspoon chicken base **or** ½ teaspoon salt
1   medium eggplant, peeled or not peeled, cut in ½ inch thick wheels
4   cups mozzarella cheese

Directions

- Preheat oven to 425 degrees
- Foil line 9 x 13 x 2 1/2 inch baking pan for easy clean up, rub olive oil onto foil.

1. Heat the water in a large sauce pan, add the oat groats. Bring to a boil, simmer 20—30 minutes or until tender but not mushy, drain and set aside.
2. Meanwhile, heat frying pan and brown the ground beef. Add the onions and continue cooking until onions are transparent.
3. Add the green pepper, garlic, okra, oregano, basil, tomatoes and chicken base, stir and bring to boil, reduce heat to medium, cook 5 minutes, stirring to blend.
4. To assemble, place oat groats in bottom of pan, pressing into the corners to form crust. Then spread sauce to cover the oat groats. Arrange eggplant over the sauce. Spoon a little sauce on top on the eggplant. Sprinkle with cheese (be sure to save enough cheese for topping). Repeat layers, and top with remaining cheese. Cover with foil. To prevent sticking, make sure foil does not touch the cheese. Bake in preheated oven for 40 minutes. Remove foil, and bake an additional 10 minutes or until eggplant is soft when pierced with a knife and top is golden and bubbly. Cool 15 minutes before serving.

To serve, have ready warmed plates. Arrange slice of mousaka in center of plate with warm crusty bread on the side.

Beef Stroganoff

Julia Child made this dish in the early 70s on her cooking show. I used to sit at my kitchen table and watch her cook as I ate lunch with my kids. What a thrill it was to see real French cooking back in the 70s.

In the 90s, when Julia was in Seattle, I had lunch with her. In my wildest dreams I never thought I'd be writing a cookbook basing a recipe on her methods. I wonder what she would think of combining eggplant and okra into beef stroganoff to say nothing of recommending oat groats instead of noodles. I think she'd be pleased with the results. Bon apetite!

Serves 4

Ingredients

1   cup oat groats, rinsed
2   cups water

1¼ pound beef sirloin cut cross grain in half inch thick strips
1   onion, thinly sliced length-wise
4   cloves garlic, minced
12   ounces (1 medium) eggplant quartered and thinly sliced
2   cups okra, frozen cut
⅛   teaspoon black pepper
2   tablespoons tomato paste
2   tablespoons dry sherry or to taste
1   teaspoon dry mustard
¼   teaspoon oregano
¼   teaspoon dill
2   cups water
1   rounded teaspoon chicken base **or** ½ teaspoon salt
3   tablespoons oat bran
½   cup sour cream

Parsley for garnish (optional)

Directions

1. Heat the water in a large sauce pan, add the oat groats. Bring to a boil, simmer 20—30 minutes or until tender but not mushy, drain and set aside.
2. Heat heavy large pot. Add the beef, dry sauté until browned, about 8 minutes. Add onions and sauté until transparent (about 2 minutes) adding a little water if needed.
3. Add the garlic, eggplant, okra, pepper, and tomato paste, stir in sherry.
4. Stir in the dry mustard, oregano, and dill.
5. Add the water, chicken base and oat bran. Stir and bring to a simmer over medium heat. Cook 20—30 minutes or until veggies are tender adding more water if needed.
6. Stir in the sour cream and heat through.

To serve, have ready warm plates. Arrange a scoop of oat groats in the center of the plate and spoon the stroganoff over the top.
Garnish with parsley if desired.

BRANDY BEEF POT ROAST

Brandy Beef Pot Roast

What a delicious treat to have an old fashioned dish with attractive aromas and hints of exquisitely executed flavor fusions. Curry leaves, NOT curry powder, contribute a subtle almost nutty flavor without overpowering the dish. The curry leaf plant (or tree if you wish), is a native of tropical Asia, southern India and Sri Lanka. Take a look online to learn more about the uses of curry leaf. It is not only for cooking but also is used medicinally.

When I cook this recipe I have to be careful to plate it up and wrap the leftovers before we sit down to eat or we'll finish it all in one sitting. George is a big pot roast fan and enjoys sandwiches made from leftovers. You'll love this version of pot roast with brandy. Brandy help tenderize the meat and adds a marvelous flavor.

Serves 4–6

Ingredients

3 - 4	pound chuck roast
1	cup brandy
1	cinnamon stick
½	cup chopped curry LEAVES* or
1	tablespoon dried crushed curry leaves
1	cup carrots, sliced
2	cups okra, cut frozen
4	large parsnips, chopped
1	medium eggplant, chopped

4	small whole potatoes
2	cups onions, chopped
4	large cloves garlic, not peeled
½	teaspoon black pepper
½	teaspoon salt (optional)
1	cup water
2	tablespoons oat bran

*Curry leaves are available at Asian stores

Directions

1. Heat a large pot or dutch oven. Place the roast into the pot, turning to brown on both sides. When brown add the brandy, scrape the bottom of the pan to loosen bits of meat, reduce heat and simmer 40—45 minutes, adding water if needed.
2. Add all ingredients except the oat bran, bring to boil, reduce to simmer and cook for 20 minutes turning meat and stirring vegetables occasionally or until meat is fork tender and vegetables are cooked.
3. When meat is done, remove from pot, place on a cutting board and let rest 10 minutes. Meanwhile, bring remaining liquid to a boil, reduce heat to simmer, then stir in the oat bran. Cook about 5 minutes or until gravy thickens adding more oat bran if needed.
4. Carefully slice the meat across the grain into ¼ inch thick slices.

To serve, have ready 4 warmed plates. Arrange meat slices on one side of the plate, place a potato next to the meat and spoon vegetables beside the potato. Remind dinner guests to shuck the garlic. (see garlic shucking)

Cooks Note: All vegetables should be cut the same thickness for even cooking. Remove cinnamon stick before serving.

Beef Mediterranean Wraps

Wraps can be such a nice change from other types of sandwiches. It's too bad they don't make a wrapper out of oats. That would be the best combination for flavor and health.

Thinly sliced roast beef from New Seasons is the best for this sandwich. They roast the beef locally with no chemicals added making it a good choice if you don't have time to roast your own beef.

Double pack the veggies into this sandwich and share it with a friend. The taste, though, is actually too good to give away even to a best friend.

Serves 4

Ingredients:

4   10 inch whole wheat tortillas

1   container guacamole dip (8 ounce container)
1   pound roasted deli beef
2   cups Mediterranean marinated roasted vegetables (see index)
2   cups thinly sliced cabbage
2   diced tomatoes
1   cup shredded cheddar cheese

Directions:

- 1 recipe Mediterranean Marinated Vegetables (see recipe index)

1. Lay the tortillas on the counter in a row. Slather the tortillas with guacamole dip. Distribute the remaining ingredients evenly on the tortillas in the order given.
2. Fold right and left sides to center, overlapping the edges. Fold the bottom edge of the tortilla up and over filling, rolling until closed with the seam on the bottom. Cut in half on the diagonal.

To serve, have ready plates with a dollop of guacamole to use for dipping. Garnish with fresh fruit.

Tex-Mex Bake

Blazing saddles? Not if you eat beans often enough. And eating beef is a good source of amino acids. Tex-Mex Bake is great hot, cold, morning. noon or night. George enjoys it for breakfast the next day. Chester can eat it too, as there are no onions in it and he eagerly awaits his dish cleaning job.

I was teaching a cooking class using the recipe and Martha, my assistant, commented that this was a can opener recipe. Counting the cans used, I chuckled and agreed. My response was simple. Using this many cans was better than using a packet of processed mix. The sodium count in the premixed packets is overwhelming. So, sharpen your can opener and enjoy the full flavors in this recipe.

Serves 6

Ingredients

Crust:
2	cups oat bran
4	cups water

Filling:
1	pound ground beef, 10% fat
2	cups eggplant
2	cups okra, frozen cut
1	green pepper, chopped
1	14.5 ounce can diced tomatoes
1	14.5 ounce can pinto beans
1	4 ounce can medium hot green chilies, chopped
1	teaspoon oregano
1	teaspoon ground cumin
1	teaspoon chicken base **or** ½ teaspoon salt
1	cup cheddar cheese, shredded

Directions

- Preheat oven to 375 degrees
- Foil line baking pan for easy clean up or rub with olive oil

Crust:
1. Fill medium sauce pan with water and bring to boil. Add oat bran, stir and simmer about 5 minutes or until water is absorbed and oat bran is soft. Pour into baking pan and spread evenly covering bottom of pan and up sides as far as it will spread.

Filling:
1. Heat a large heavy saucepan. Crumble the ground beef in the pan and cook over medium high heat until brown. Pour off fat. Add the rest of the ingredients **except** the cheese and cook 5 minutes or until it bubbles.
2. Pour the filling on top of the oat bran crust. Sprinkle cheese over the top and cover with foil.
3. Bake at 375 degrees 40 minutes or until it begins to bubble around the edges. remove foil and bake uncovered 10 minutes or until golden brown. Let stand 15 minutes.

To serve, arrange slice on warm plate.

Beef Chardonnay

Beef Chardonnay could be made with burgundy. Red wine gives me an instant headache so I avoid it. Many of the recipes reflect my personal food intolerances. My dad had many food intolerances which used to annoy me growing up. I even accused him of doing it on purpose. Revenge for my intolerance to his food intolerances set in at about age 35 and the list began to grow slowly. First, I couldn't eat lobster, then wheat began to bother me and the list gained momentum as time went by. But, I'm thankful I can still enjoy this. No matter if you use burgundy or chardonnay, you will love this scrumptious flavor combination.

Serves 4

Ingredients:

1   cup oat groats, rinsed
2   cups water

1½ pounds beef round steak, cut in one inch cubes
2   cups chopped onion
4   cloves garlic, whole or chopped
1   cup chardonnay
1   cup water
½   teaspoon chicken base **or** ½ teaspoon salt
1   teaspoon savory
1   teaspoon black pepper
1   teaspoon red pepper flakes (optional)
1   medium eggplant quartered and cut in ½ inch thick slices
2   cups okra, frozen cut
4   carrots, peeled cut in half inch thick slices
1   cup thinly sliced mushrooms
3   tablespoons oat bran

Directions:

1. Fill a medium sauce pan with water and add the rinsed oat groats. Bring to a boil, reduce heat and simmer 30 minutes or until tender.
2. Heat a large heavy pot. Dry sauté the beef until browned, add the onions and cook until slightly browned and liquid is gone. Add water, scrape the bottom of the pan and stir.
3. Add the remaining ingredients and stir. Bring to a boil, reduce heat and simmer 30 minutes or until meat is fork tender and vegetables are cooked.

To serve, have ready warmed plates. Arrange some oat groats in the center of each plate and spoon the meat and vegetables over the top and serve immediately.
A nice crusty bread is a great accompaniment along with a glass of chilled chardonnay wine.

Mustard Beef Short Ribs

Toss the garlic cloves in not peeled and let the diners "shuck the garlic" as they devour this mouth watering dish. Don't be alarmed by the use of plain ol' yellow mustard. It produces the flavor of fine wine while tenderizing the meat. The recipe is the result of being out of nearly everything that would tenderize the meat. George saw the mustard and thought we were having burgers. When I placed this dish in front of him he couldn't believe yellow mustard could produce such a fine flavor. Mopping up the gravy with some down home corn bread topped off the meal. This hearty dish is a shoe-in for pleasure packed eating.

Serves 4

Ingredients

4   pounds beef short ribs

Marinade:
1/3 cup prepared yellow mustard
1   tablespoon lemon juice
1   tablespoon sugar
½   teaspoon salt
½   teaspoon black pepper
1   clove garlic, minced

3   cups water
1   medium eggplant, chopped
     (about 2 cups)
2   cups okra, frozen cut
½   medium onion, chopped
1   medium tomato, quartered
4   cloves whole garlic not
     peeled

Directions

- Preheat oven to 350 degrees
- Use pot on stove that can go in oven
1. To marinate the beef short ribs, place the ribs in a zip lock bag large enough to hold the ribs. In a small bowl, combine the mustard, lemon juice, sugar, salt, black pepper and garlic. Pour marinade over the ribs in the bag, squeeze the air out of the bag and manipulate the bag to coat the ribs. Marinate in refrigerator 2 hours or over night.
2. Heat a large heavy pot, add the ribs and dry sauté over medium heat. When a nice brown color gravy has formed from browning the ribs, add water and scrape bits off bottom of the pan, then add the eggplant, okra, onion, tomato and garlic.
3. Cover the pot and place in the oven. Bake 2 hours stirring and turning the ribs occasionally. Bake until meat is fork tender. Remove from the oven. Skim off fat before serving.

To serve, have ready warmed plates. Serve the ribs with vegetables spooned over the top. Add a warm piece of cornbread on the side if desired.

BEEF – LAMB
GYRO

Beef – Lamb Gyro

While I was working for the Archdiocese of Chicago Food Service (later the name was changed), a similar recipe was menued to use USDA commodities. At the time, there was an overabundance of beef in the system which necessitated clever ways to take advantage of it. Or course, there was no okra, but tons of salt was included in their recipe because it had to mimic popular fast food in the Chicago area. Traditional gyros are made with lamb. You could use all ground lamb if desired.

Serves 4 – 6

Ingredients:

Cucumber Sauce
½ cucumber, finely chopped
¼ teaspoon granulated garlic powder
¾ cup plain yogurt

Gyro Meat
1½ cups onion chunks
4 large cloves peeled garlic
2 cups okra, frozen cut
8 ounces ground beef
8 ounces ground lamb

2 tablespoons oregano
¾ tablespoons black pepper
1 tablespoon thyme
½ teaspoon salt
4 – 6 whole wheat pita bread

Topping:
2 cups chopped cabbage
2 medium diced tomatoes
or Mediterranean Marinated Vegetables
(see index for recipe)

Directions

- Preheat oven to 350 degrees
- Foil line baking pan for easy clean up

Cucumber sauce:

1. In a small bowl place the finely chopped cucumber. Add the yogurt and stir in the garlic powder. Mix well and let stand to marry flavors.

Gyro meat

1. In a food processor using steel knife blade, place the onions and garlic. Process 10 seconds. Add the okra and process tuning on and off to mince okra, scraping down sides of processor.
2. In a large bowl place the beef and lamb. Add the onions, garlic okra, oregano, pepper thyme and salt, mix well by hand.
3. Form mixture into 6 patties. Place on a sheet pan. (Use disposable gloves or rinse hands frequently with cold water.) Bake 40 minutes or until done and juice runs clear when knife is inserted. Cool thoroughly before trying to lift off the pan.

To serve, toast pita bread on stove top burner flipping often until toasted. Cut pita bread in half, place half of patty in each piece or place on top of toasted pita and serve openface style. Use Mediterranean marinated veggies or cabbage and tomato for topping. Drizzle on cucumber sauce.

Chicken

KFC Style Fried Chicken
Crispy Chicken Paprika
Chicken Gumbo
Pumpkin Chicken
Leggie Chicken
Chicken in Green Tea with Wild Wasabi
Turkey 5 Spice Roll Up
French Country Chicken Thighs
Sesame Chicken Soup
Orange Juicy Chicken
Chicken & Pasta Thai Style

KFC Style Fried Chicken

Serving fried chicken is a pleasing meal any time. The batter for the chicken boasts a nutty flavor and adds a nutritional wallop. I used this recipe in one of my cooking classes resulting in a resounding cry from the students, "This is better than Popeye's!" The added surprise of the side dish beat out mashed potatoes for flavor and appeal. This could be considered a fusion of flavors from Asia with the Scottish highland kick from the oat bran.

Serves 4

Ingredients:

1   whole fryer cut into serving size pieces or 8 chicken thighs or legs
¼   cup sesame oil or olive oil

Breading:
1½ cups oat bran
½   teaspoon each:
      curry powder
      salt
      cumin, ground
      ginger, ground
      allspice, ground

Side Dish (Asian Branolenta) Measure leftover breading mixture and place in small sauce pan. Add water twice the amount of breading mixture. Bring to boil, reduce heat to simmer and cook about 5 minutes.

Directions:

- Preheat oven to 425 degrees
- Foil line baking pan for easy clean up.
1. In large plastic bag or bowl mix together the oat bran, curry, salt, cumin, ginger and allspice.
2. Pour oil into baking dish, swirl to cover the bottom of the dish.
3. Dredge the chicken in the bran mixture. Place the chicken pieces on a sheet pan, turn chicken to coat with oil. Bake 20 minutes, turn and bake another 20 minutes or until juices run clear when knife is inserted into the thickest part of the meat.

To serve, arrange chicken on warm plate and spoon a helping of Asian branolenta next to chicken. A cucumber salad and glass of white wine completes the meal.

Cooks Note: If crust starts to brown too much, cover the chicken loosely with a sheet of aluminum foil and continue baking. The chicken can also be fried on top of the stove.

Every time I prepare this dish memories of my Aunt Marge emerge. When I was about ten, she took me to a Hungarian restaurant. We had a dish similar to this, but the topper was dessert. Aunt Marge ordered a shot of Drambuie for me. It arrived in a small footed sugar rimmed glass. The waitress placed it in front of me and with a flick of a match set it on fire. I was awe struck. The perfect ending to a meal with paprika.

Paprika has other spellings and is sometimes called paprikash. There are many flavors of paprika such as sweet, Hungarian, hot, mild, chicken and smoked to name a few of the ones I've come across. I love the crispy crunch of this dish with chicken crumbles sprinkled on top as a garnish. Complete the meal with cole slaw and a robust wine or flaming Drambuie.

Crispy Chicken Paprika

Serves 4

Ingredients

1	cup oat groats, rinsed
2	cups water
1	whole chicken breast with skin on
1	cup thinly sliced onions
2	cups water
1	chopped tomato
2	cups eggplant peeled and cut into one inch cubes
4	leaves finely sliced kale

2	cups okra, frozen cut
½	sliced green pepper
2	teaspoons chicken base **or** ½ teaspoon salt
2	tablespoons paprika or to taste
½	cup Brown Cow brand creamy top plain yogurt
2	tablespoons sour cream

Directions

1. In a small saucepan combine the oat groats and water. Bring to boil, reduce heat and simmer 20—30 minutes or until tender. Drain and set aside.
2. Skin the chicken breast and reserve skin, then cut the breast meat into 4 portions.
3. Heat a large heavy pot or dutch oven and fry the chicken skin over medium heat until crispy taking care not to get spattered by hot grease. When skin is crispy, drain on paper towel. Cut into crumbles and set aside. Pour off the fat from the pan, then dry sauté the onions until soft. Add the water.
4. Turn the heat to high and add the tomato and eggplant, kale, okra, green pepper, chicken base and paprika. Bring to boil, reduce heat to simmer and cover. Cook about 15 minutes then add the chicken pieces. Cook until the chicken turns white and veggies are tender about 20 minutes depending on size of chicken breasts. Cook uncovered until reduce liquid by half. Stir in the yogurt and the sour cream, heat and serve. Do not boil or yogurt will curdle.

To serve, have ready warm plates. Arrange oat groats on one side of plate, add a piece of chicken and spoon on vegetables. Sprinkle chicken crumbles on top.

Chicken Gumbo

There is one rule that both the Creoles and Cajuns agree upon and that is that there is no one rule and no one recipe when it comes to matters of food. Gumbos come filled with a variety of vegetables and meat or seafood. You'll find this recipe filled with good flavor and good health.

File' powder is ground sassafras . It can be found at some Fred Meyers. The very best source I've found outside N'Orleans is the Butterfly Herb shop in Missoula, Montana. http://www.butterflyherbs.com/ or call them to order 406-728-8780

Serves 4

Ingredients

1 recipe cooked oat groats (see index for recipe)

1 large onion, chopped
1 medium green pepper, chopped

4 ounces andouille sausage
2 boneless chicken breasts, cut in one inch chunks*

2 15 ounce cans diced tomatoes
1 15 ounce can tomato sauce
½ medium eggplant, peeled and chopped
2 cups okra (half of a pound bag)
4 cloves garlic not peeled (shuck at the table)
2 tablespoons Lea & Perrins Worcestershire sauce
2 tablespoons Louisiana Hot Sauce or to taste
2 tablespoons chicken base

4 tablespoons *file` powder spice or to taste

Directions

- Prepare one recipe of oat groats. Set aside and keep warm.
1. While the oat groats are cooking, heat a large heavy pot and dry sauté the sausage, when cooked, remove the sausage from the pot and drain the grease. Then add the chicken chunks and cook until white all the way through, then remove from pot, set aside and keep warm.
2. Add the onions and brown, add a little water if needed, then add the green pepper, diced tomatoes, tomato sauce, eggplant and okra, stir. Bring to boil, reduce heat to simmer.
3. Stir in the Worcestershire sauce, hot sauce and chicken base. Cover and continue to simmer about 20 minutes or until the eggplant is tender.
4. Add back the sausage and chicken. Stir, then sprinkle file` powder over top and gently stir in, bring back to boil, reduce heat and simmer 5 minutes adding a little water if needed. Taste and adjust seasonings.

To serve, have ready warm bowls. Place a scoop of oat groats in bowl. Ladle gumbo over the oat groats, sprinkle cracklins on top and add crusty warm bread on the side.

The spectacular fusion of Chinese 5 spice combined with south of the border flavors gives this union of cultures a scrumptious flair. Cook the chicken the day before using the Leggie Chicken Soup recipe (see index). Shred the chicken while warm for ease of preparation. The pumpkin pumps in some vitamin A along with flavors that enhance the health benefits.

The first time I prepared this recipe the taste was delicious, but it looked like a plop on a plate. If that happens to you, serve it in a bowl and enjoy a bottle of pumpkin ale* with it.

Serves 4–6

*Pumpkin ale is available seasonally from Buffalo Bills's Brewery. Google for more info.

Pumpkin Chicken

Ingredients

10 6 inch corn tortillas
Filling:
1   pound cooked shredded chicken (light or dark meat)
2   cups eggplant, medium chopped
2   cups okra, frozen cut (half of one pound bag)
1   teaspoon Chinese 5 spice seasoning

Sauce:

1   15 ounce can pumpkin puree
1   15 ounce can water
1   teaspoon chili powder
½   teaspoon cumin
2   teaspoons chicken base **or** ½ teaspoon salt
¼   teaspoon black pepper
4   cloves minced garlic
2   teaspoons tabasco sauce

Topping:
8   ounces shredded sharp cheddar cheese

Directions

• Preheat oven to 325 degrees for glass baking dish or 350 degrees for metal baking pan.
• Foil line baking pan for easy clean up.
Filling:
1. In a medium sized skillet dry sauté the eggplant and okra. Stir in the Chinese 5 spice seasoning. Mix in the shredded chicken, keep warm.
2. Sauce:
   In a medium size saucepan combine and bring to boil, the pumpkin, water, chili powder, cumin, chicken base, black pepper, garlic and tabasco sauce. Reduce heat and simmer 5 minutes.
3. Into a baking dish ladle a little sauce to barely cover the bottom. Layer the tortillas, chicken and vegetable mixture and then sauce. Continue to layer in the same manner, then top with cheese. Cover the pan with aluminum foil. Bake covered 30 minutes. Then, uncover and bake until the cheese is melted and sauce is bubbly about 10 minutes. Let rest 15 minutes before cutting.

To serve, have ready warmed plates, arrange a portion on a plate or serve in warm bowl. Add a salad to the meal if desired.

Leave the skin on the garlic and enjoy "garlic shucking" at the table. It adds interest, is a conversation starter and a time saver when preparing. Leggie Chicken Soup is a very basic soup recipe with endless flavor possibilities. It's difficult to think of a vegetable that wouldn't go well in this soup.

To give it a Southwest zest toss in some chili powder and cumin. Looking for a French accent? Then tarragon's the ticket. Flavoring soup with curry and garam masala could bring fantasies of shopping in an open air market in old Bombay. Rosemary and thyme is a reminder of cooking on the plains. Experiment with your favorite herbs and spices to create your own signature soup.

Leggie Chicken Soup

Serves 4

Ingredients

4   whole chicken legs, skin on
1   chopped onion
2   rounded teaspoons chicken base **or** 1 teaspoon salt

4   cloves garlic not peeled
1   cup chopped carrots
2   stalks chopped celery
1   medium eggplant, about 2 cups not peeled
2   cups okra, frozen cut (half of on pound bag)

Flavor soup with favorite herbs and spices. See story above.

Directions

1. Remove the chicken skin from the legs. Heat a large heavy pot. Fry the skin on medium heat until crispy. Be careful of grease spatters. Remove, drain on paper towel. Cut into crumbles and set aside.
2. Pour off the grease from the pan and add onions. Dry sauté until golden brown.
3. Add the chicken legs, chicken base and enough water to cover. Heat to a simmer until meat begins to separate from the bones.
4. Remove the chicken legs from the pot, cool until able to handle easily. To the pot add enough water to make about four cups of liquid to cook the vegetables. Add the garlic, carrots, celery, eggplant, and okra, stir, heat to simmer and cook 20—30 minutes or until vegetables are tender.
5. Meanwhile, detach the meat from the bones, cut into bite sized pieces and return to soup when vegetables are cooked.

To serve, have ready warmed soup bowls. Ladle soup into bowls and serve immediately.

Chicken in Green Tea with Wild Wasabi

Just saying, "WASABI," gives a thrill. Wasabi is a Japanese horseradish that is used as condiment for sashimi (raw seafood) and sushi. The fusion of chicken and tea with wasabi on the side is a great lunch dish. The fragrance of the tea and a touch of wasabi will create a relaxing meal with enough punch to get you back on your feet and ready for the afternoon.

Adding wasabi powder to the dish while cooking doesn't give the expected punch. Wasabi powder is best when made into a paste by mixing with a little water and served on the side. With its wild name and zinging taste, wasabi should be considered part of your menu on a regular basis. Wasabi provides wonderful health benefits especially if you have a cold or sinus problems.

It's nice to keep wasabi around in the powdered form and reconstitute it as needed, but fresh is always better. Either way, it's a great addition to your meals.

Serves 4

Ingredients

1	cups oat groats, rinsed
2	cups water
2	tablespoons wasabi powder
2	skinless chicken breasts
1	cup water
1	teaspoon chicken base **or** ½ teaspoon salt
1	tablespoon sesame seeds
4	cups hot freshly brewed green tea

Directions

1. In a small saucepan combine the oat groats and water. Bring to boil, reduce heat, cover and simmer 20 minutes or until tender. Drain and set aside.
2. Heat water in a large heavy pot, stir in the chicken base and add the chicken. Bring to simmer over medium heat. Cook about 20 minutes or until the chicken is cooked through. The chicken should be be white all the way through. Remove the chicken from pot. Cool enough to handle. Cut into bite sized pieces, set aside and keep warm.
3. While chicken and oat groats are cooking, do the following:

- Reconstitute the wasabi powder in a small bowl using enough water to make a paste and set aside.
- Heat small skillet, add the sesame seeds and toast until golden brown. Set aside.
- Prepare the tea according to package directions.

To serve, have ready warm soup bowls. Distribute oat groats evenly into bowls. Spoon chicken over oat groats and pour in the tea. Sprinkle toasted sesame seeds on top. Serve wasabi as a condiment in a separate dish.

Turkey 5 Spice Roll-Up

Notice the use of cabbage in the roll up instead of lettuce? Pascual, my son-in-law, who is from a small town in Central Mexico told me they never used iceberg lettuce when he was growing up. Cabbage was traditional in his home town. He laughs and says that only gringos eat iceberg lettuce.

The vitamins and minerals in cabbage are far greater than lettuce. Plus, it has better staying power and does not get soggy like lettuce does.

Serves 4

Ingredients

2   pounds turkey legs or thighs
1   stick cinnamon
1   tablespoon Chinese 5 spice
4   cloves garlic
1   medium onion, quartered
1   tablespoon chicken base **or** ½ teaspoon salt

Water

1   cup chopped onion
1   cup okra, frozen cut
1   cup finely sliced kale
3   cups peeled chopped eggplant
1   teaspoon ground sage
¾   cup cranberry juice
1   cup dry white wine
1   cup water

½   can whole cranberry jelly
2   cups thinly sliced cabbage
4   10 inch flour tortillas

Tip: Roll-up can be sliced in half to serve.

Directions

1. In a large heavy saucepan place the turkey parts and cover with cold water. Add the cinnamon stick, Chinese 5 spice, garlic, onion, and chicken base. Bring to a simmer over medium heat and cook for 30 minutes or until the meat begins to separate from the bone. Remove the turkey from the pot. When cool enough to handle, pull meat off of the bones, cut into bite sized pieces, set aside and keep warm.
2. Heat a large heavy skillet and dry sauté the onion until transparent.
3. Add the okra, kale, Swiss chard, eggplant, sage, cranberry juice, wine and water. Bring to boil, reduce heat and simmer until liquid is reduced and nearly gone. Stir in turkey pieces.
4. To assemble the sandwich, slather whole cranberry sauce on tortilla. Spoon on the turkey mixture and top with cabbage leaving enough room around the edges to wrap and fold without being too full. Fold right and left sides to center overlapping edges. Fold bottom edge of tortilla up and over filling, rolling until closed with the seam on the bottom. Cut in half if desired.

French Country Chicken Thighs

When I was growing up, chicken was a premium meat and was only served on Sundays or special occasions. Gradually chicken became a less expensive meat and more available for 29¢ a pound. The availability of chicken parts soon followed. Dark meat was never considered a prize and has continued to be less expensive. The meat from legs and thighs can be substituted in most recipes that call for chicken breasts.

My husband and I saved money for our first house by eating chicken and tuna fish. We used to eat it to save money, now we eat it to save our health.

A word of caution about frying the chicken skin separately to use as a garnish. Don't get carried away and eat it while cooking the rest of the meal! It's mighty tasty and adds a nice crunch.

Serves 4

Ingredients

1   recipe branolenta (see recipe index)

4   chicken thighs, skin on
1   14.5 ounce can diced tomatoes in juice
1   6 ounce can tomato paste
1   cup water
1   teaspoon chicken base* **or** ½ teaspoon salt
2   teaspoons basil
2   teaspoons oregano
¼   teaspoon red pepper flakes (optional)
½   14 ounce bag frozen sliced sweet peppers
12 ounces (2 cups) 1 inch cubes eggplant, peeled or not peeled
2   cups okra, frozen cut
1   2 ounce can sliced black olives
4   thinly sliced kale leaves

* Chicken base (see index)

Cooks Note: Branolenta is a delicious way to get some extra bran into your diet.

Directions

1. Remove the skin from the chicken thighs. Heat a large heavy skillet. Fry the skin on medium heat until crispy. Be careful of grease spatters. Drain on paper towels. Break into crumbles and set aside.
2. Heat a separate large heavy pot or Dutch oven. Brown the skinned chicken thighs over medium heat adding a little water to loosen from bottom of pot as needed. While the chicken is browning, prepare the branolenta.
3. When the chicken thighs are browned, add the tomatoes, tomato paste, water, basil, chicken base, oregano, red pepper flakes and stir.
4. Add the sliced sweet peppers, eggplant, okra, olives and kale, gently stir, cover and cook on medium heat 20 – 30 minutes or until veggies are tender. Add water if needed.

To serve, have ready warm bowls. Place a scoop of branolenta on a warm plate, top with a chicken thigh and spoon vegetables on top. Garnish with crispy chicken crumbles.

Sesame Chicken Soup

Give meaning to a chilly winter meal with Sesame Chicken Soup. Use it as a main course or a delicious small serving at the beginning of a meal. This recipe was particularly fun to develop. It all started because I had some squash to use up. I had gone to a Japanese fall festival where farmers brought vegetables to sell. Squash were 50¢ each. So, I bought enough to carry me though the winter.

While looking around the pantry, I noticed some of the squash needed to be used. A recipe began to form in my head. Next, Chester and I walked out to the garden to pick some kale that was still alive in January. The rest of the ingredients were quickly assembled from the kitchen food stash. Thank the technology gods, the chicken was quickly defrosted in the microwave and the squash cooked all in a matter of minutes. This recipe could also be made with leftovers. Either way, brightly colored squash can make a meal sparkle.

Serves 4

Ingredients

¼   cup sesame seeds toasted

2   slices chopped lean bacon, fat trimmed
½   medium onion, diced
1   whole boneless skinless chicken breast cut in ½ inch chunks

4   leaves finely sliced kale
1   cup peeled eggplant, thinly sliced in 1 inch square pieces
1   cup okra, frozen cut
½   cup water

1   quart whole milk
1   can cream style corn
1   cup butternut squash, cooked, one inch cubes

¼   cup oat bran
Toasted sesame oil

Directions

1. Heat a small skillet then add the sesame seeds and toast over medium heat, set aside.
2. In a large heavy pot, dry sauté the bacon, drain on paper towel, set aside. In same pot, dry sauté the onions. Add the chicken pieces and dry sauté until chicken browns a little and turns white on the inside.
3. Add water, scrape the bits off the bottom of the skillet, then add the kale, okra and eggplant, simmer about 10 minutes or until vegetables are tender.
4. Slowly pour in the milk, stir and scrape bottom of pan. Add can of creamed corn, squash and cooked bacon, stir.
5. Sprinkle the oat bran over top and stir in. Over medium heat, bring to simmer and cook about 5 minutes or until the soup is thickened. Do not boil or milk may curdle.

To serve, have ready warmed soup bowls. Ladle soup into bowls, add a tiny drop of toasted sesame oil on top and sprinkle with toasted sesame seeds.

Chicken & Pasta Thai Style

Don't get excited about the calories in the coconut milk. If you eat the correct portion, it will be ok. Remember portion control should always be lurking to keep you from yourself. Nothing is better than a 1/2 cup of ice cream unless it's the entire quart. No, no! Put it back and behave yourself and you can eat anything – just not too much. Whew, I need to read that over and over...

Save a trip to a Thai restaurant and make this dish yourself. The refreshing zip from the red curry paste will send a welcome message to your taste buds.

Instead of using the dry sauté method, this recipe does need a little (very little) sesame oil to bring out the flavor. If possible, use fresh Thai basil to give this dish the zest of Thailand. Chester eagerly awaits the opportunity to lick the emptied coconut milk can. I have to make sure to wipe his muzzle after he licks the can clean or he'll use the drapes for a napkin.

Serves 4

Ingredients:

1 cup cooked oat groats
 or
 1/3 pound pasta (bow tie pasta pictured)

1 teaspoon toasted sesame oil
½ pound ground chicken
1½ teaspoons red curry paste

½ cup water
12 ounces eggplant (2 cups), peeled and cut in small cubes
2 cups okra, frozen cut
½ green pepper, medium chopped
½ onion, medium chopped
20 fresh basil leaves or 1 teaspoon dried

1 13.5 ounce can coconut milk
1½ tablespoons fish sauce (available in Asian markets)
1 teaspoon each:
 Kikoman soy sauce
 sugar
 rice vinegar

• Fresh chopped cilantro for garnish (optional)

Directions:

• Cook oat groats (see recipe index) or cook pasta according to package directions.
1. Heat a large saucepan with sesame oil, then add the chicken and sauté until it starts to brown. Then, stir in curry paste and cook about one minute.
2. Add water, stir and scrape bottom of pan. Add the eggplant, okra, green pepper, onion and basil leaves, cover and cook about 8 minutes or until the eggplant is soft.
3. Add the the coconut milk, fish sauce, soy sauce, sugar and vinegar. Stir and heat just until it starts to bubble.

To serve, place scoop of pasta or oat groats into warm bowl, ladle chicken and veggies on top. Garnish with chopped cilantro.

Cooks Note: Eggplant must be fully cooked, but the rest of the veggies can be tender crisp.

Orange Juicy Chicken

I love this for a 'brunchie' type meal. The cheery color and flavor lends itself well to bridal or baby showers. But don't sell it short for a regular supper. If you're up for a treat, this is a good one.

A little Triple Sec on the rocks as you cook sets the spirit of fine dining while sticking to lowering your cholesterol. The added crunch of cracklings made from the chicken skin is a snappy garnish. Feels naughty, but it's nice!

Serves 4

Ingredients

2   whole chicken breasts, skin on
    or 4 chicken legs or thighs
2   tablespoons water or more if needed
1   cup dry white wine
4   cloves thinly sliced garlic
½   medium onion, chopped
1   medium peeled eggplant, coarsely chopped
2   cups okra, frozen cut (half of a one pound bag)
2   teaspoons chicken base **or** 1 teaspoon salt

1   12 ounce can orange juice concentrate
½   cup Triple Sec liquor
1   Roma tomato, quartered length wise

Directions

•   Preheat oven to 375 degrees for metal pan or 350 degrees for glass baking dish.
1. Remove the skin from the chicken thighs. Heat large heavy skillet, fry the skin on medium heat until crispy. Be careful of grease spatters. Remove the crispy skin from the skillet and drain on paper towels. Cut into crumbles and reserve.
2. In the same skillet, pour off the fat, brown the chicken pieces, then transfer to a baking pan.
3. To the skillet add the water and sauté the garlic and onions briefly, about 2 minutes. Add the wine, eggplant, okra, chicken base, orange juice and Triple Sec, stir and bring to boil. Immediately pour over chicken in baking pan. Lay tomato quarters across the top, cover with foil and bake 40 minutes or until chicken is fork tender and veggies are cooked.

To serve, cut chicken into serving size pieces, place on warm plates and spoon vegetables and sauce over the top. A scoop of rice or oat groats on the side would complete the meal nicely.

111

LAMB

**Lamb Shanks with Crispy Branolenta
Lamb Shanks, Kumquat Sauce
and Pomegranate Oat Groats
Lamb Stew Swedish Style**

Lamb Shanks with Crispy Branolenta

This is a brilliant recipe and especially tasty served over a slice of branolenta (see index for recipe). I like branolenta as well as or better than polenta as it provides the opportunity to eat bran at a different time of day. For a little variety when preparing the branolenta, add some hot chilli peppers to give it some zip.

The first time my mother fixed lamb I remember commenting that it smelled like the neighbors' dirty house. I was told to either eat it or go hungry. I went hungry and didn't touch lamb until I grew up and learned to cook it myself. Lamb has been bred to be very mild unlike the lamb years ago. I wonder what I would think of Mother's lamb now.

Serves 2

Ingredients

1 recipe bra-
 nolenta (see
 recipe index)
 cut in wedges
 and fried

2 lamb shanks,
 fat trimmed

1 medium on-
 ion, chopped

1 cup dry white
 wine

1 cup water

1 teaspoon chicken base **or** ½
 teaspoon salt

3 cups peeled eggplant,
 chopped

1 cup sliced carrot, fresh or
 frozen

1 cup okra, frozen cut

1 cup sliced mushrooms

4 cloves garlic, whole (shuck at
 table)

1 teaspoon each:
 thyme, marjoram, rosemary

½ teaspoon black
 pepper or to taste

1 bay leaf, if desired

• olive oil to fry
 branolenta wedges

Directions

• Prepare one recipe of branolenta and pour into lined 8 inch round cake pan.

1. Heat a large heavy pot, dry sauté the lamb shanks until brown. Pour off the fat if needed. Add the onion and brown adding a little white wine to loosen the onions from pan. Cook about 30 minutes. When the shanks and onions reach a rich golden brown color, add the water, chicken base and remainder of wine. Bring to boil, reduce heat to simmer, cook 30 minutes.

2. Add the rest of the ingredients. Bring back to boil, reduce heat to simmer, cook about 30 minutes or until the vegetables are tender.

3. While the lamb shanks and vegetables are cooking, in a small skillet heat one teaspoon olive oil and fry the wedges of branolenta until a little crispy on the edges.

To serve, remove bay leaf and place lamb shank on warm plate next to a wedge of fried branolenta, add vegetables on the side of the plate forming a triangle.

Lamb Shanks, Kumquat Sauce and Pomegranate Oat Groats

Now there's a mouthful that's delicious. Succulent lamb shanks accompanied by oat groats embedded with kale and pomegranates, finished with a kumquat honey sauce.

It's just too bad oat groats don't have a better name. Until now they have hidden their beauty and rustic hardiness. Tossing in kale and pomegranates makes oat groats a dish to set before anyone, even a king. Then, adding a couple of spoons of kumquat sauce sets this dish apart.

Serves 4

Ingredients

4   lamb shanks, trimmed
½   teaspoon pepper
6   cups water
3   tablespoons chicken base or
     1½ teaspoons salt
2   onions, chopped
3   cups peeled eggplant, chopped
2   cups okra
3   tablespoons mild curry powder
1½ teaspoons ground ginger
½   teaspoon saffron threads

Kumquat Sauce:
16   kumquats, halved or quar-
     tered, seeds removed
3   tablespoons honey
1/3 cup water
1   teaspoon lemon juice

Oat groats with pomegranates
2   cups water
1   cup oat groats, rinsed
½   teaspoon chicken base or ½
     teaspoon salt
4   large thinly sliced kale leaves
1   cup pomegranate seeds

Directions

- Preheat oven to 350 degrees

1. In a large heavy ovenproof pot dry sauté the lamb shanks until golden brown about 15 minutes. Transfer shanks to a plate and set aside.
2. Pour off any fat. Return pot to high heat and add the water then stir in the chicken base. Scrape bits off the bottom of the pot. Add the onions, eggplant, okra, curry powder, ginger, and saffron, bring to boil, reduce heat to simmer.
3. Add back the lamb shanks, cover the pot and place in the oven. Bake about 1½ hours or until the lamb is tender but not falling off the bone. Turn the lamb halfway through baking. Add water if needed.

Kumquat Sauce
1. In medium sauce pan place kumquats, honey, water and lemon juice. Bring to boil, reduce heat to simmer. Stirring, reduce liquid by half and cook until kumquats are soft, about 10 minutes.

Oat Groats with Pomegranates
1. In medium saucepan, combine water, oat groats, chicken base and kale, stir. Bring to boil, reduce heat and cover. Cook about 30 minutes or until oat groats are tender.
2. Just before serving, stir in the pomegranates.

To serve, arrange lamb shank next to scoop of oat groats and pomegranates and spoon kumquat sauce over lamb shank.

Lamb Stew Swedish Style

The fragrant aroma of this dish will call to you as it simmers on the stove. Lamb Stew Swedish Style could be made with lingonberries instead of cranberries to make this a more authentic Scandinavian dish. Cranberries are more available, less expensive and a wonderful substitute.

Coffee and cranberry juice sound like a most unusual combination but work well to enhance the overall flavor and texture.
This would be delish served over oat groats or rice.

Serves 4

Ingredients

Marinade
1½ cups coffee, freshly brewed
1   cup cranberry juice
2   tablespoons half & half*
1   tablespoon sugar
2   tablespoons cognac
2   cloves minced garlic

1   pound lamb stew meat, trimmed
3   cups peeled eggplant, chopped in one inch cubes
2   cups okra, frozen cut
1   Jewel variety sweet potato, chopped in one inch cubes
1   tablespoon oat bran
       (add more if thicker sauce is desired)

*The half & half will curdle when mixed with the cranberry juice. Don't worry about it as the tender curds add to the flavor.

Directions

1. In a large zip lock bag combine the coffee, cranberry juice, half & half, sugar, cognac, and garlic. Add lamb and marinate 2 hours or overnight.
2. Heat a large heavy pot, dry sauté the lamb. Add the marinade, eggplant, okra, and sweet potato, stir. Bring to boil and reduce heat to simmer and cook about 40 minutes or until veggies are soft and meat is fork tender.
3. Stir in the oat bran and cook about 5 minutes to thicken the gravy.

To serve, have ready warmed plates. If serving lamb over oat groats, arrange some oat groats in center of each plate and ladle lamb stew on top.

PORK

Pork Goolosh with Sauerkraut
Pork Leche with Apples
Pork Chops with Kalamata Olives
Pork with Shredded Ginger
Pork Dijon
Italian White Tie Pasta

Pork Goolosh with Sauerkraut
(Correct spelling goulaush, goulouch, goulasch)

Looking up the spelling of goulouch was an interesting exercise. There seems to be several spelling variations allowing, you to choose the spelling you like.

Prepare this recipe on faith. The first time I developed and cooked this recipe, George said, "I'm glad you didn't ask me if I wanted this because I would have said NO. But, this is REALLY good."

Lest I digress, let's talk about the sauerkraut. It's important to use a brand of sauerkraut like Bubbies because it is shredded, salted and cured for several weeks in huge wooden vats with no added chemicals like other brands use. Remember, the more natural a food is, the better for you.

Don't forget to taste the sauerkraut before putting it in the recipe. If it's too salty, put it in a colander and rinse with cold water.

A mouth watering serving of aromatic oat groats, a salad of dark greens and a glass of wine completes this delectable meal.

Serves 4

Ingredients

Oat Groats
1   cup oat groats, rinsed
3   cups water
1/3 cup Del Monte ketchup*

2   pounds lean pork cut in 2 inch strips (boneless country ribs)
1   cup chopped onions
2   cups eggplant cut in 2 inch chunks
1   cup okra, frozen cut
1   25 ounce jar Bubbies sauerkraut
¼   cup Del Monte ketchup
1   cup water
1   tablespoon caraway seeds (more or less as you desire)

Other brands of ketchup can be used but the flavor may not be as good.

Directions

1. In a medium sized saucepan combine the oat groats, water and ketchup. Bring to boil, reduce heat and simmer about 30 minutes or until soft but not mushy. Drain.
2. Meanwhile, heat a large heavy pot and dry sauté the pork strips until brown. Add the onion, eggplant, okra, sauerkraut, ketchup, water and caraway seeds, bring to boil, reduce heat to simmer and cook about 30 minutes or until pork is tender.

Serve on warmed plates. Spoon the pork and vegetables on top of a bed of oat groats in the center of the plate.

Cooks Note: Use any cut of pork for this recipe. Be sure to trim off the fat. I like country ribs because they are economical. Look for locally grown organic pork.

Pork Leche with Apples

Milk, pork and apples? Never heard of such a thing? You're not alone. The first time I cooked this recipe I knew I had to watch the pan closely so it didn't burn. Did I listen to my own advice? Nope, so "Watch the pot so it doesn't burn!"

It's definitely worth the trouble to cook this dish. Imagine getting vitamin A, K, calcium, and potassium, to name a few, in each delicious bite.

If you prefer a sweeter flavor, use a sweeter apple. The tartness of the Granny Smith adds a nice contrast to the other ingredients. This is one of the few dishes where I added salt. It can be cooked without if you please, but you'd have to bring the flavor up by cooking the meat a little darker but NOT burned.

Serves 4

Ingredients:

Marinade:

- 1   cup onions sliced ¼ inch thick
- 4   cloves sliced garlic
- 2   Granny Smith apples, cored and chopped
- 1   sliced carrot
- ½   teaspoon salt
- ¼   teaspoon black pepper
- 1   teaspoon thyme
- 1   medium peeled eggplant, chopped
- 2   cups okra, frozen cut (half of 16 ounce bag)
- 3   cups milk

- 1   pound lean country ribs or pork loin roast

Directions:

To marinate:

1. In a large zip lock bag combine the onions, garlic, apples, carrot, salt, pepper, thyme, eggplant, okra and milk. Marinate 2 hours or overnight in the refrigerate, turning the bag occasionally.

To cook:

1. In a large heavy pot dry sauté the meat until brown. Pour off the fat. Add 1 cup of liquid from the marinade and cook on low heat about 30 minutes, taking care it doesn't burn. Scrape the bottom of pan often.

2. Add the rest of the marinade liquid and vegetables. Cook over low heat until vegetables are tender and the milk forms a gravy, about 20 minutes.

A rich nutty thick sauce should have formed. Remove the meat and let rest. Slice into serving size portions.

To serve, have ready warm plates. If serving the pork with oat groats, arrange some oat groats on one side of plate with the pork next to the oat groats. Spoon vegetables over the oat groats. Drizzle some gravy over the pork and serve immediately.

Cooks Note: This does burn easily, so be sure to cook over low heat and watch carefully. It's worth the trouble. The milk will curdle, but that's part of what makes the gravy delicious.

Pork Chops with Kalamata Olives

The golden seared meat and tang of Kalamata olives are brimming with good flavor Soon it will be one of your favorite comfort foods. Any cut of pork chop can be used. My favorite is the center cut but a less expensive cut can turn out to be a bonus.

Serves 4

Ingredients

4   pork chops 1 inch thick, trimmed
¼   cup dry white wine
1   14.5 ounce canned S&W brand diced tomatoes in juice
2   teaspoons minced garlic

2   cups okra, frozen cut
1   cup eggplant, peeled and cut into 1 inch cubes
½   cup kalamata olives, cut in half

Directions

1. Heat a large heavy skillet. Dry sauté the pork chops until brown and cooked through, about 12 minutes on each side using medium heat. Remove and keep warm.
2. Drain the fat from the pan. Add the wine and let sizzle a little. Add the tomatoes, including juice, garlic, eggplant, okra, and olives. Bring to boil, reduce heat and simmer for about 30 minutes or until the eggplant is tender. Arrange pork chops on top of the vegetables. Cook about 5 minutes.

To serve, have ready warm plates. Arrange pork chops on plate and surround with vegetables. Drizzle a little juice over the pork chops. A slice of crispy branolenta would make a great addition. (See index for recipe)

Cooks Note: Add more wine if vegetables get too dry while cooking.

Pork with Shredded Ginger

This recipe contains many of the flavors and fragrances—ginger and sesame oil—I associate with the Silk Road. There are many varieties of sesame oil. Some are touted as high temp, toasted, and virgin to name a few. Try different types and brands and decide for yourself. I prefer the heavy flavor of the toasted sesame oil and use the "high temp" for frying.

Serves 4

Ingredients

1 cups oat groats, rinsed
2 cups water

2 tablespoons "high temp" sesame oil
¼ cup shredded fresh ginger,
1 teaspoon Kikoman soy sauce
1 teaspoon minced garlic
1 pound pork, cut in 1 inch strips

2 cups peeled eggplant, cut in 1 inch chunks
1 cup okra, frozen cut (half of one pound bag)
1½ tablespoons fish sauce*
1½ teaspoons soy sauce
½ teaspoon sugar

½ cup sliced fresh carrots
½ medium onion, sliced lengthwise
1 cup whole green beans
½ cup water
1 tablespoon oat bran

Garnish:
Cut green onions lengthwise into three-inch strips.

Available in Asian markets.

Directions

1. In a small saucepan combine the oat groats and water. Bring to boil, reduce heat and simmer 20—30 minutes or until tender. Drain and set aside.
2. Heat a wok or heavy skillet and pour in the oil. Add the ginger, soy sauce and garlic. Stir fry until fragrant.
3. Add the pork and cook until the pork turns a whitish color.
4. Stir in the eggplant and okra, cover and cook until eggplant is tender about, 5–10 minutes.
5. Add the fish sauce, soy sauce and sugar, stirring.
6. Bring to simmer. Stir in the carrots, onions, green beans, water, and oat bran. Stir continuously and cook until the vegetables are tender crisp and the oat bran has thickened the "gravy," about 3–5 minutes.

To serve, have ready warm plates or bowls. Serve on top of oat groats and garnish with green onions.

Pork Dijon

What a dainty dish to set before the king or anyone else. Delicate flavor that finishes with a slight "bite" on the end. This would be a great make ahead dish that could be served to guests or family. Add a side dish of oat groats with a little gravy spooned over the top. Don't forget the all important dark green leafy salad with some fresh carrots.

It's important to get as many orange veggies as possible included in your food intake. Studies have been done that suggest carrots and other orange veggies help keep eyes healthy and sightful.

Serves 4

Ingredients

1   whole pork tenderloin

Marinade:
1   tablespoon Bubbies horseradish
¼   cup Dijon mustard
2   tablespoons Worcestershire sauce
2   tablespoons fresh lemon juice
1   teaspoon pepper
1   teaspoon lemon zest

1/3 cup water
2   tablespoons oat bran
1   cup water (to rinse marinade bag)
1   medium eggplant, chopped (about 2 cups)
2   cups okra, frozen cut
1   cup onions, chopped (1 medium)
4   cloves garlic (if desired, not peeled, to shuck when eating)
4   whole wheat pita bread

Directions

1. To marinate the pork, place the pork in zip lock bag large enough to hold the pork and marinade. In a separate bowl blend the horseradish, mustard, Worcestershire sauce, lemon juice, pepper and lemon zest. Pour over the pork in the zip lock bag and marinate in refrigerator at least 2 hours or overnight.

2. To cook, heat a large heavy pot or Dutch oven. Dry sauté the pork until browned. Add 1/3 cup water and the oat bran.

3. Into the zip lock bag that held the marinade, add 1 cup water, swish around to mix, and pour into the pot.

4. Add the eggplant, okra, onion and garlic, bring to boil, reduce heat and simmer 30 minutes or until veggies are tender.

5. Remove the pork from pan and place on cutting board. Let rest about 5 minutes, then slice into desired thickness.

6. Grill the pita bread on the stove burner, flipping often until toasty.

To serve, have ready warm plates. With bread flat lay meat and veggies on one half and fold over to eat. Or place meat and veggie on plate and serve with warm pita bread. Naan bread or tortillas can also be used.

Italian White Tie Pasta

4-H introduced me to Italian cuisine. In the 50's, the then famous tv chef, Francis Pope (pronounced Fran-sue-aah) gave my 4-H club a cooking lesson. He showed up in a navy blue suit and spoke with an Italian accent. No chef hat for him or even an apron. He cooked in the navy blue suit and had his assistant do anything that might mess up his suit. Our mothers snickered later about needing an assistant to help at home.

We were thrilled to taste the foreign, mysterious dish. Unusual herbs like oregano and basil wafted through the air as he measured the ingredients. I'll never forget the aroma and flavor of my first Italian food. This recipe is inspired by my 4-H recipes.

Serves 4

Ingredients:

1	pound bow tie pasta
1	pound organic Italian sausage
1	tablespoon basil
1	tablespoon oregano
1	tablespoon ground fennel seeds
2	cups Mediterranean style roasted vegetables (see index for recipe)
½	cup oat bran
4	cups milk
4	whole wheat pita bread, grilled (optional)

Directions:

- Cook the bow tie pasta according to the package directions
1. In a heavy skillet or deep saucepan brown the sausage. Pour off the grease.
2. Stir in the basil, oregano, fennel and oat bran. Add the roasted vegetables, oat bran and milk. Stir and scrape the pan. Bring to simmer stirring occasionally until thickened, about 6–8 minutes.

To serve, have ready warm plates. Place the pasta in the center of the plate with grilled whole wheat pita bread on the side. Cover pasta with vegetable sausage mix.

Cooks Note: Oat groats or branolenta can be used instead of pasta.

SEAFOOD

Tasty Tuna Stuffed Peppers
Smart 'n' Elegant Seafood Salad
Seafood Gumbo
Deep Sea Delight 'n' Scotch Pudding
Encrusted Salmon Dijon

Smart 'n' Elegant Seafood Salad

Elegant, low calorie and delicious for dinner or lunch. The crispy chow mein noodles add a nice crunch, but they do have calories. If you're trying to cut down on calories, you may want to eliminate them or savor just a few.

Broccoli is the near perfect vitamin source. I like to include broccoli as often as possible in meals or snacks. This recipe is appealing year round, but the summer seems a more likely time To serve, it. Set a tall glass of homemade lemonade or a chilled glass of your favorite wine next to this dish as the mouth watering goodness calls you to the table.

Smart 'n' Elegant Seafood Salad

Ingredients

1	medium eggplant with skin on, sliced into ½ inch thick wheels
1	teaspoon salt
1	pound cooked crab meat or pollock
1	cup broccoli florets
½	medium red onion, thinly sliced
½	cup minced red bell pepper
½	cup chopped cucumbers
2	cups mixed salad greens

Dressing:
½	cup mayonnaise
1	teaspoon toasted sesame oil
2	tablespoons sugar
2	tablespoons rice vinegar
2	teaspoons garam masala
2	tablespoons water

Garnish:
1	cup crunchy chow mein noodles
4	tablespoons candied ginger, finely chopped
8	cooked shrimp for garnish if desired

Directions

1. Heat a medium saucepan and fill with one inch of water. Add the salt and slices of eggplant. Bring to boil, reduce heat, cover and simmer 6–8 minutes or until tender but not mushy. Shock* in cold water to chill, drain and set aside.
2. Select nice pieces of seafood (cooked shrimp is pictured) to be used as garnish, set aside.
3. In a small bowl whisk together the mayonnaise, sesame oil, sugar, vinegar, garam masala and water.
4. In a large bowl place the seafood, broccoli, onion, pepper, cucumber and salad greens. Then pour the dressing over the top and gently mix.

*Shock in cold water means to drain the eggplant and place it in ice cold water to stop the cooking.

To serve, have ready chilled plates. Arrange eggplant in center of the dish, distribute the salad evenly and sprinkle chow mein noodles around the edge of salad. Garnish with pieces of the reserved seafood and finish with a sprinkling of candied ginger.

Cooks Note: Garam masala is an Indian spice. Apple cider vinegar can be substituted for rice vinegar if desired.

Tasty Tuna Stuffed Peppers

In the 70s I worked in a grocery store. Green peppers cost the same as they do today in the winter if they were available. Adjusting for inflation, that would make them $7 or $8 a pound back then.

One winter afternoon while working my shift at the grocery store, my neighbor Florence, came through my check-out lane. Florence put four green peppers up on the counter and I expressed my surprise at her spending so much money. She gave me a tight smile, sighed and then told me that she had wanted to take a small vacation. Her husband said N.O. So, instead of a vacation she decided to make stuffed peppers for dinner to enjoy a little extravagance. Peppers are still a little spendy in the winter. So, treat yourself to a mini vacation and enjoy this recipe.

Serves 4–6

Ingredients:

6   peppers cored and seeded (red, green or yellow)
2   cups peeled eggplant chopped small
2   cups okra, frozen cut (half a one pound bag)
2   tablespoons water

2   6 ounce cans tuna, drained
1   15 ounce can diced fire roasted tomatoes*
¼   cup oat bran
½   cup green olives, pitted w/pimentos
4   cloves minced garlic
2   tablespoons capers, rinsed and minced
2   teaspoons basil
1   teaspoon pepper

Water

*Any kind of canned tomatoes can be used.

Directions:

- Preheat oven to 325 degrees for glass pan. 350 degrees for metal pan.
1. In a large saucepan, place the eggplant, and add one inch of water. Bring water to a boil, reduce heat to a simmer and cook about 8–10 minutes or until eggplant is tender. Drain and set aside.
2. In large bowl combine the tuna, tomatoes, oat bran olives, garlic, capers, basil and pepper.
3. Mix in the cooked eggplant and okra.
4. Stuff the peppers with the tuna mixture and place in a baking pan.
5. Pour enough water into the bottom of the baking dish to fill one quarter inch high. Cover and bake about 40–50 minutes or until the peppers are tender.

To serve, have ready warm plates. Arrange one pepper on a plate. Serve with favorite cole slaw or tossed salad.

Cooks Note: This works best in a regular oven. Cooking in a microwave varies from oven to oven, making it difficult to give accurate directions for cooking time.

Seafood Gumbo

You would call this dish one of the finest N'Orleans feasts. Set a piece of warm crusty bread next to the bowl of gumbo, pour a glass of 3 or 4 buck Chuck and you're on it...(Charles Shaw wine) found at Trader Joes.

File' powder is ground sassafras. It can be found at some Fred Meyers. The very best source I've found outside N'Orleans is the Butterfly Herb shop in Missoula, Montana. http://www.butterflyherbs.com/ Take a look at their website, then call them to order 406-728-8780.

Serves 4

Ingredients

1   cups oat groats, rinsed
2   cups water

4   ounces andouille sausage cut in one inch slices

1   large onion, medium chopped
1   medium green pepper, medium chopped

1   14.5 ounce can diced tomatoes
1   14.5 ounce can tomato sauce
½   medium size eggplant (2 cups), peeled or not peeled chopped one inch chunks
2   cups okra
2   tablespoons Lea & Perins Worcestershire sauce
2   tablespoons Louisiana Hot Sauce or to taste
2   tablespoons chicken base

1   pound white fish cut in one inch chunks or any seafood assortment desired
4   tablespoons file` powder spice*

*Pronounced fee lay.

Directions

1. In a small saucepan combine the oat groats and water. Bring to boil, reduce heat and simmer 20—30 minutes or until tender. Drain and set aside.
2. While the oat groats are cooking, heat a large heavy pot and dry sauté the sausage. Pour off the grease.
3. Add the onions and brown, then add the green pepper, diced tomatoes, tomato sauce, eggplant and okra, stir. Bring to a boil, reduce heat to simmer.
4. Stir in the Worcestershire sauce, hot sauce and chicken base. Continue to simmer, cover and cook 30 minutes or until eggplant is tender.
5. Stir in the seafood and cook about 5 minutes or until the seafood is white all the way through. Sprinkle file` powder over the top and gently stir in, bring back to boil, reduce heat and simmer 5 minutes adding a little water if needed. Taste and adjust the seasonings.

To serve, have ready warm bowls. Place a scoop of oat groats in the bowl then ladle gumbo over the top, add crusty warm bread on the side.

Cooks Note: The amount of file` spice can be adjusted to your taste. Serve file` on the side in case guests would enjoy more.

Deep Sea Delight 'n' Scotch Pudding

Amazing, simply amazing! This dish will knock your socks off. You won't believe the goodness of this combination. It's spicy, yet the crispy outside gives way to the delightful flavor of freshly caught fish.

Soaking the fish in milk is the key to reviving freshness. Adding booze to the okra lends undertones of the exotic while balancing the silky elegance of the okra in the side dish of savory Scotch Pudding.

Serves 4

Ingredients

Marinade:
1 pound pollock filets cut into portion size pieces
Milk enough to cover fish

Coating Mixture:
1 package instant butterscotch pudding mix
1 cup oat bran
2 teaspoons cayenne pepper

Toasted "high temp" sesame oil

Directions

To marinate:
1. In a large zip lock bag place pollock and add enough milk to cover. Refrigerate and marinate 20 minutes or overnight.

To cook fish:
1. In another large zip lock bag combine the pudding mix, oat bran and pepper. Place fish in the mixture, shake gently to coat. Let rest while large skillet is heating.

2. In a heated large skillet, pour enough sesame oil to cover the bottom of the pan about ¼ inch deep.
3. Gently add pieces of fish and cook about 7 minutes on each side until golden brown, adding more oil if needed. While fish is cooking, make the pudding and keep warm.

Scotch Pudding

Ingredients

2 cups okra, frozen cut
2 cups water
Remaining coating mix

1 small tomato, chopped
½ cup scotch whiskey

Directions

1. Heat a medium saucepan and add the whisky, okra, water and coating mixture, bring to boil, reduce heat and stir constantly until thickened to oatmeal consistency, about 8 minutes.
2. When the pudding is thickened, stir in the tomatoes.

To serve, have ready warm plates. Arrange fish on side of plate and spoon pudding next to the fish. Garnish if desired.

Cooks Note: Amount of water used in pudding should be twice the amount of coating mixture. Example: 1 cup coating mixture needs 2 cups water.

Encrusted Salmon Dijon with Crispy Coconut Eggplant

The American Heart Association recommends two six-ounce servings of fish each week, especially oily fish.[1] Salmon is considered to be on the "good list" of fish. Salmon lends itself to salads and is delicious just baked or broiled.

A tiny bite of zing from the Dijon mustard and the juicy goodness inside the crispy coating will make your heart jump with joy. You may prefer to use a lighter oil or bake the dish with olive oil drizzled over the top.

[1] http://www.americanheart.org/presenter.jhtml?identifier=4627

Serves 4

Ingredients:

1　recipe Crispy Coconut Eggplant (see index for recipe)

Marinade:
1　pound salmon filets cut into portion size pieces
Milk enough to cover fish
2　tablespoons Dijon mustard or more if needed

Coating:
1　cup oat bran
½　teaspoon salt
½　teaspoon black pepper

Toasted "high temp" sesame oil for frying
Garnish: Lemon wedges if desired.

Savory Dinner Pudding:
1. Measure the left-over coating for the fish.
2. Measure the left over milk plus enough water to equal twice the amount of the coating mixture
3. In a medium saucepan combine the coating mixture, milk and water and bring to boil. Reduce heat and simmer 5 minutes or until mixture thickens to the consistency of oatmeal.

Directions:

To marinate:
1. In a large zip lock bag place the salmon and enough milk to cover. Refrigerate and marinate 20 minutes or over night.

---

1. Prepare the recipe of Crispy Coconut Eggplant. While eggplant cooks, remove the salmon pieces from the marinade, then spoon on Dijon mustard to thinly coat. Set aside.
2. In a large zip lock bag combine the pudding mix, oat bran, salt and pepper. Place the fish in the mixture, shake gently to coat. Let rest while skillet is heating.
3. In the heated skillet pour enough sesame oil to cover the bottom of the pan about ¼ inch deep.
4. Gently add the pieces of fish and cook about 7 minutes or until golden brown. Turn the fish and cook another 7 minutes or until golden brown and desired doneness has been reached. Add more oil as needed.
5. Meanwhile, cook eggplant according to the recipe.

Baking method: On a foil lined sheet pan arrange the breaded fish, drizzle oil over the top, bake at 375 degrees until golden, about 15 minutes. Turn the fish and bake another 15 minutes or until a crispy golden crust has formed or desired doneness has been reached. See cooks note.

To serve, have ready warm plates. Arrange salmon on warm plate on top of eggplant, spoon savory pudding along side. Garnish with lemon wedge.

Cooks Note: Cooking time for the fish depends on the thickness of the fish, sacrifice a piece to test by

VEGETARIAN

Pizza Stuffed Eggplant
Spaghetti Sauced Branolenta
Swimming Angel
Okra Scramble

Pizza Stuffed Eggplant

Pizza stuffed eggplant is the next best thing to pizza. No need to call Dominoes ever again. Forget Pizza Hut. Have a glass of Chianti or your favorite beverage when you dig in. The aroma of oregano, intense undertones of basil, concentrated scents of tomatoes and inviting bits of garlic bring the perfect balance to this dish. Prep time is quick once you get the hang of it.

It's also delicious reheated, cold or pack it for lunch. Cut into small chunks and add it to an omelette the next day. You'll find this a pleasant repast no matter when, where or how you eat it.

Serves 4

Ingredients:

2	small eggplants or one large enough to cut into four servings
1	small onion, diced
½	red pepper, diced
3	cloves garlic, minced
2	cups okra, frozen cut
2	tomatoes, diced
1	teaspoon basil
1	teaspoon oregano
¼	cup oat bran
1	large egg
8	ounces mozzarella cheese shredded
6	pepperoni slices

Directions:

- Preheat oven to 350 degrees
- Foil line baking pan for easy clean up

1. Slice the eggplant in half lengthwise, scoop out and save center leaving enough meat inside skin so it holds its shape when baked. Boil skin about 10 minutes or until soft but firm enough to handle. Set aside.
2. While the skin is cooking, dry sauté the onion and the scooped out eggplant pieces. Remove from heat. Allow to cool.
3. Add the red pepper, garlic, okra, tomatoes, basil, oregano and bran. Stir, then add the egg and mix.
4. Fill the eggplant shells with mixture, sprinkle on mozzarella cheese, top with slices of pepperoni. Make a tent from aluminum foil and cover. Bake at 350 degrees 40–50 minutes. Time will vary depending on size of eggplant. Insert knife in eggplant to test for doneness. Adjust time accordingly. Leave uncovered last 10 minutes of baking to brown. Let rest for 15 minutes to set before cutting.

To serve, cut into serving sizes and place on warm plate. Add some crusty bread and a glass of chilled wine.

Spaghetti Sauced Branolenta

All the pleasure of having an Italian style meal without pasta or meat. If you don't eat wheat or try to stay gluten free, this will be an even bigger delight for you. Or, if you love crusty bread and want to use your calories by dipping bread in the sauce, this is your ticket. A nice glass of red or white wine if you please, maybe a favorite movie to watch, what could be better?

Serves 4

Ingredients

1   recipe branolenta (see index for recipe)

4   one inch thick slices of whole eggplant, skin on

1   cup chopped onion
1   cup white wine

4   cloves garlic
½   cup green pepper
4   large leaves kale, thinly sliced
2   cups okra, frozen cut
1   2.2 ounce can sliced black olives

1   14.5 ounce can S&W brand diced tomatoes in juice
1   6 ounce can tomato paste

1   teaspoon basil
1   teaspoon oregano
¼   teaspoon red pepper flakes
½   teaspoon liquid smoke
1   teaspoon honey

Directions

- Prepare one recipe of branolenta, set aside and keep warm.
1. In a large saucepan place the eggplant, add one inch of water. Bring water to a boil, reduce heat to a simmer and cook about 8–10 minutes or until tender but not mushy. Remove, drain, set aside and keep warm.
2. Heat a large heavy skillet, dry sauté the onion until golden. Add wine, let sizzle and stir.
3. Add the garlic, green pepper, kale, okra, and olives, stir.
4. Pour in the can of tomatoes, add tomato paste, stir and blend. Bring to boil, then reduce heat to low simmer.
5. Add the basil, oregano, and pepper flakes, stir. Add the liquid smoke and honey. Stir and simmer on low about 20–30 minutes to allow flavors to marry.
6. While the sauce cooks, slice the branolenta into serving size pieces. Heat the skillet, add enough olive oil to cover the bottom of the skillet. Place slices of branolenta in heated skillet and fry until golden brown turning as needed about 8 - 10 minutes.

To serve, have ready warm plates. Arrange the eggplant in center of the plate and ladle vegetables over the top with a wedge of branolenta on the side.

Swimming Angel

Swimming Angel is adapted from a recipe I came across on the website of Uwajimaya, an Asian grocery store in Portland, Oregon. The recipe called for Thai peanut sauce.

I thought about peanuts and okra, two crops originally from Africa that followed the Silk Road from Africa to Thailand and eventually made their way to America. Thai peanut sauce and okra intrigued me enough to develop this recipe into a gourmet fusion of good health and good taste.

Contrary to popular myth, coconut milk does not transform into bad cholesterol that clogs arteries. Coconut milk is made from crushed coconut and contributes calcium, iron, magnesium, and potassium to your nutrition needs. Nearly one third of the world's population depends on coconut to some degree for their food and economy.
(www.coconutresearchcenter.org)
Serves 4

Ingredients:

- 1 medium eggplant, peeled and sliced in ½ inch thick wheels
- • Water
- 2 cups chicken cut in 1/2 inch slices
- 2 13.5 ounce cans Chaokoh brand coconut milk
- 1 medium onion, cut in half and sliced lengthwise
- 2 cups okra, frozen cut
- 4 asparagus spears cut on the diagonal in 1 inch long pieces
- 1 teaspoon ground fresh chili paste
- 2 handfulls fresh spinach

Garnish:
Warmed Thai Accents brand peanut sauce (optional).

2 tablespoons chopped peanuts for garnish (optional).

Directions:

1. In a large saucepan place the eggplant, pour in 2 inches of water and cover. Bring to boil, reduce heat to simmer and cook until eggplant is tender but not mushy about 8 minutes. Remove eggplant from pan with a slotted spoon, drain and set aside.

2. Using the same pan and hot water, add the onions, okra, asparagus and chili paste. Add enough water to cover vegetables, heat to boiling, reduce heat to simmer and cook about 10 minutes or until okra is soft.

3. Add the chicken slices and coconut milk, bring back to simmer and continue simmering until the chicken turns white. Stir in the spinach and let stand until ready to serve.

To serve, have ready warmed soup bowls. Arrange one eggplant wheel in each bowl. Ladle in soup and top with a dash of peanut sauce. Add a sprinkle of chopped peanuts.

Cooks Note: Eggplant: only 4–6 slices are needed for this recipe. Eggplant can be peeled if desired. All of the eggplant can be cooked and the unused portion frozen.

Okra Scramble

Great for a breakfast, lunch or dinner. The egg cuts the silky threads of the okra and makes an awesome meal. Mother Nature gave us the egg as a means to get a perfect protein.

For years eggs have been given a bad rap, but that's changed. Eggs are good for you and they do not give you high cholesterol as believed.

Nutrition Research Center.org, referring to the latest research, stated that eggs fall into the good fat category. Clare M. Hasler, Ph.D, University of Illinois, stated, "...it is now known that there is little if any connection between dietary cholesterol and blood cholesterol levels....eggs are an excellent dietary source of many essential (e.g., protein, choline) and non-essential (e.g., lutein/zeaxanthin) components which may promote optimal health."

ref.:http://nutritionresearchcenter.org/healthnews/eggs-are-they-good-or-bad-for-you/

Serves 4

Ingredients:

½   teaspoon butter
½   cup okra, chopped*
1   clove minced garlic

6   large eggs

1   cup fresh spinach, chopped
1   small tomato, diced
1/3 cup gorgonzola or blue cheese, crumbled

* partially defrost okra, then chop

Directions:

1. Heat a large skillet (10-inch) preferably non-stick over medium heat. Add the okra and garlic stirring until golden brown, about 5 minutes.
2. Meanwhile in a large bowl whisk the eggs until blended. Then, add to the hot skillet and cook the eggs over medium low heat until they begin to set on the bottom. Add spinach, stir and cook until nearly set. Add the tomatoes, stir and cook until the tomatoes are warmed, about one minute.

To serve, have ready warm plates. Arrange a portion attractively on the plate. Sprinkle with crumbled gorgonzola cheese.

Cooks Note: Sliced apples or apple sauce makes a nice addition to this meal.

Food Sources

Barbur World Foods
9845 SW Barbur Blvd
Portland, OR 97219
503-244-0670

Butterfly Herb
Missoula,Montana. http://
www.butterflyherbs.com/
406-728-8780

Bob's Red Mill Whole Grain Store
5000 SE International Way
Milwaukie , OR 97222
503 607-6455
Toll Free: 800 553-2258
www.bobsredmill.com/

Cash & Carry
731 SE Stephens St,
Portland,OR
503-232-7157

1420 NW 14th Avenue,
Portland, OR -
503-221-1049

910 North Hayden
Meadows Drive,
503-289-1022

Fubonn Shopping Center
2850 SE 82nd Avenue
Portland, OR 97266

Market of Choice
8502 SW Terwilliger
Portland, OR 97219
503-892-7331

Uwajimaya Inc.
10500 SW Beaverton
 Hillsdale Hwy.
Beaverton, OR 97005
www.uwajimaya.com
503-643-4512

Chicken Base

Classic Gourmet brand chicken base is used in many recipes. I find this brand to give a nicely flavored chicken broth. It is available at Cash & Carry in the Portland, Oregon area.

It can be added to sauces, gravies, dips and cooking liquids for oat groats, rice or vegetables. If you can't find it in your area, contact Ventura Foods 1-800-VENTURA. It is a food service item and is not available in retail stores. It's well worth the trouble to find it as it gives food that professional touch and deep flavor with a similar flavor profile of home made stock. It is one of the few prepared food items I have in my kitchen.

Index

Index

Index

Index

Jacobus Rinse Mixture for *Heart Disease*

By: Miles Hassell MD,
Internal Medicine, Comprehensive Risk Reduction Clinic
St Vincent Hospital, Portland, OR.

The idea of including the Rinse mixture as a supplement to my heart disease treatment program is an exception to my general policy of sticking to well-studied ideas. This one is based on mainly anecdotal evidence, but I consider it worth trying.

Who was Jacobus Rinse?

The late Jacobus Rinse was a Dutch industrial chemist who came up with an odd combination of nutritional ingredients as a treatment for atherosclerosis after developing heart disease himself. He used this mixture on himself for 16 years, and during that time had no more symptoms of heart disease.

He decided that maybe his mixture worked, and wrote about it in the chemical journal 'American Laboratory' in July 1973. It was popularized by a variety of authors in the 1970s and '80s, which led to many people trying it out.

What does the Rinse mixture do?

The reason we include it here, despite the lack of corroborating scientific trial data, is that patients who use the Rinse mixture seem to do very well with respect to their heart disease. They often have large drops in their LDL cholesterol, and frequently comment that their arthritic joints feel better.

So, based on nothing more than a hunch that Jacobus Rinse was onto something, I developed an improved (and simpler) version. Dr. Rinse's original formula was 2 teaspoons brewer's yeast, 2 teaspoons lecithin granules, 2 teaspoons raw wheat germ, ½ teaspoon bone meal, 1 tablespoon soy oil, and 1 tablespoon yogurt. I have taken the liberty of modifying the recipe based on my own research. I have retained the brewer's yeast, as we now know that these yeasts contain variable amounts of statin com-

Rinse Mixture (Miles' version)

I suggest you use this daily for 2 months, and then check your cholesterol panel to see if it works for you.

(Daily quantity)

2 teaspoons brewer's yeast
2 teaspoons lecithin granules
4 tablespoons oat bran

1. Blend ingredients together and add mixture into cereal or yogurt, or anything else in order to make it tasty. Some people add it to smoothies but I prefer it stirred into ½ cup of unsweetened applesauce.

2. For larger batches, store in an airtight container in the refrigerator.

pounds, the most potent cholesterol lowering chemicals in use.

Brewer's yeast is a rich source of protein, minerals such as selenium and chromium, B vitamins, and nucleic acids. I generally prefer it to the milder product called 'nutritional yeast' because brewer's yeast seems to have a better nutrient profile. (Brewer's yeast is a 'dead' yeast, and cannot multiply in your body or cause yeast infections.)

Look for brewer's yeast in the nutrition section of your local supermarket. Some brands taste pretty pungent; I like the Lewis Labs brand[1], but any of them are fine as long as you tolerate them.
[1]www.lewis-labs.com

Lecithin granules are extracted from a number of sources, most commonly soybeans or egg yolks, and are available at natural food stores.

Possible Rinse side effects
Some patients have noticed increased bowel movements and gas. If you experience these symptoms, try cutting the dose in half and gradually work up to the full dose. Also try eating the mixture at meal time.

Copied with permission from:
Good Food Great Medicine Cookbook

Comparison of
Nutritional Brewers Yeast and Brewers Yeast

Nutritional Brewers Yeast			Brewers Yeast		
RED STAR 16 grams*			Lewis Labs 30 grams**		
Thiamin (B1)	9.6 mg	640%	Thiamin	1.2 mg	80%
Riboflavin (B2)	9.6 mg	565%	Riboflavin	1.5 mg	90%
Niacin	56 mg	280%	Niacin	10 mg	50%
Vitamin B6	9.6 mg	480%	Vitamin B6	0.8 mg	40%
Vitamin B12	8 mcg	133%	Vitamin B12	0.03mcg	5%
Folate	~	~	Folate	60	15%
Folic Acid	240 mcg	60%	Folic Acid	~	~
Calcium	11.2 mg	1%	Calcium	0 mg	0%
Iron	0.77 mg	4%	Iron	1.1 mg	6%
Magnesium	20.8 mg	5%	Magnesium	32 mg	8%
Phosphorus	174.4 mg	17%	Phosphorus	0 mg	0%
Potassium	320 mg	9%	Potassium	633 mg	18%
Sodium	5.12 mg	0%	Sodium	63 mg	3%
Zinc	3.2 mg	21%	Zinc	1.5 mg	10%
Copper	0.128 mg	6%	Copper	1 mg	50%
Manganese	0.094 mg	5%	Manganese	~	~
Selenium	22.4 mcg	32%	Selenium	63 mcg	90%
Chromium	<.05	0%	Chromium	n/a	140%

*Red Star® brand yeast provided data to: www.bulkfoods.com/nutritional_yeast.htm

**Lewis Labs nutrition data provided to: www.nutritiondata.com/facts/custom/1323569/2